their

faces

shone

*A foster parent's lessons
on loving and letting go*

their
faces
shone

*A foster parent's lessons
on loving and letting go*

Kate H. Rademacher

Light Messages

Durham, NC

Published 2020 by Light Messages Publishing
www.lightmessages.com
Durham, NC 27713 USA
SAN: 920-9298

Paperback ISBN: 978-1-61153-333-0
E-book ISBN: 978-1-61153-343-9
Library of Congress Control Number: 2020936921

To Peanut
and her family

And to my parents, Bruce and Lynn Holbein,
who were there from the beginning

Names and details of some of the stories have been changed to protect the identities and privacy of people involved.

Moses came down from Mount Sinai. As he came down from the mountain with the two tablets of the covenant in his hand, Moses did not know that the skin of his face shone because he had been talking with God.

—(Exodus 34:29)

Prologue

THE TECHNICIAN AND I LOOKED TOGETHER at the grainy image on the screen. I held my body still. She made some adjustments, trying to get the blurry gray lines to come into greater focus. We both watched and waited. Would the image be clear enough? Had she gotten it?

I was at the sheriff's department on a Friday afternoon. They were taking fingerprints so they could run state and federal criminal background checks on me. They no longer used messy ink; it was all digital, and the woman running the machine explained that it can be tricky to capture a detailed image that is clear enough to process. My oversized prints appeared on the computer monitor, fuzzy and almost unrecognizable at first. Like a sonogram that provides a hard-to-decipher window into new life, the image on the screen provided a hazy glimpse of what might be a beginning for our family. This moment was key to a new child coming into our lives; fingerprinting was a critical step in becoming licensed as foster parents. The social worker had explained that the state might proceed with processing our application if some of the other required paperwork was incomplete, but no placement would be made without a set of state-certified prints. They wouldn't place a child in any home without running exhaustive background checks.

This wasn't how I expected it would be. I had hoped that when we were expecting another child, I would be flat on my back, waiting to have an ultrasound image interpreted, like any other parent-to-be. Instead, the clerk at the sheriff's office grunted, "Twist your pinky finger slightly more to the left. That's it. Right, that's good. Got it."

Nothing about this experience was what I expected. I hadn't predicted the endless series of concerned questions from family and friends *(Did I really know what I was getting myself into?)* I hadn't anticipated the multiple rounds of screening interviews with social workers instead of baby showers and late-night review sessions with my husband of *What to Expect When You're Expecting.* I hadn't expected that I would be putting my family at risk when I brought a new child into our home. Our daughter, Lila, had just turned eight that month. She was a sweet, perceptive, funny, tender person, and my husband and I loved her beyond any rational measure. During our first home visit to become licensed as foster parents, the social worker warned us that children who have been abused or neglected sometimes act out in horrific ways, even the youngest kids. Just the month before, a five-year-old in foster care had sexually abused the biological child of the foster family—their seven-year-old daughter.

So why was I here? Why was I sitting on a grimy chair in Hillsborough, North Carolina, while a woman twisted my fingers and wrist into painful contortions? Did it just reflect my stubborn refusal to accept the limitations in my life, my inability to recognize that I couldn't "have it all?" Or was this entire journey somehow—in ways I didn't yet understand—a God-filled call? If we'd dusted the scene, would we have found God's fingerprints all over this situation? At that point, I wasn't sure. All I knew was that if we said yes to this experience, our lives would unquestionably be changed. When you sign up to become a foster parent, you never know how long a child will be in your home. You don't know if or when they'll call you. When they do call, you typically have just a few hours to decide if you'll accept the placement, because if you're not willing to take the kid, the caseworker must contact the next person on her list. There were so many unknowns; all I hoped was that by taking this step, our lives wouldn't be thrown into chaos.

The woman at the sheriff's office clicked the mouse, and the image on the monitor froze. She had gotten it. The image was clear enough to process. I signed the consent form. The prints would be released for screening. We were on our way.

PART ONE

Preparation

1

Decisions

I GOT THE EMAIL JUST A FEW DAYS BEFORE I left for Addis Ababa, Ethiopia. An elevated alert for terrorist activity had been issued by the State Department. Several weeks before, two would-be suicide bombers in Ethiopia's capital city had accidentally detonated a bomb in their apartment; if it had reached its intended target, it would have gone off during the World Cup qualifying soccer game against Nigeria. Just a few months before, a tragic terrorist siege in a Kenyan shopping mall had left almost seventy dead. The same Somali group who had claimed responsibility in Kenya had announced that Addis Ababa was one of its next intended targets. According to the email, the threat was to be taken seriously. In Kenya, they had issued a similar warning before the attack.

It was twelve months before I had my fingerprints taken at the sheriff's office. A group of colleagues and I were traveling to East Africa for work later that week. Two thousand people were gathering in the Ethiopian capital for an important public health conference. For the past six years, I had been working for a large international non-governmental organization that promoted increased access to birth control in developing countries. The meeting that would take place in Addis Ababa was a major biannual event in our field. Prominent leaders—including influential donors and government officials—were scheduled to attend. Security would be tight, but everyone was still concerned.

As I read the email the organizers sent a few days before the conference began, the potential threat of violence they described felt distant and theoretical to me. Something unreal and far away, even though we would depart for Addis Ababa in less than thirty-six hours. A colleague and friend who had lived in Kenya and spent weekends browsing in the mall where nationals and ex-pats had been gunned down experienced it differently. The lines around her eyes and mouth revealed the strain and the emotion she felt as we prepared for our trip.

But for me, the trip was a chance to travel to one of the ancient heartlands of Christianity. Several years earlier, I had converted to Christianity and been baptized in the Episcopal church in my hometown of Chapel Hill, North Carolina. Now, this was a precious opportunity to visit one of the first countries where Christianity had taken root. Philip's conversion of an Ethiopian court official is documented in the New Testament (Acts 8: 26-40), and in the fourth century, the king of Ethiopia declared Christianity the state religion. Today, over thirty-five million people belong to the Ethiopian Orthodox Church. The night we arrived, a loud crooning prayer was being broadcast from a church nearby, the sound reverberating against our hotel walls until the early hours of the morning. My sleep-deprived colleagues complained about it at breakfast, while I rocked in my seat, hands tucked beneath my thighs. I was itching to visit that church to check it out for myself.

Yet the updated travel advisory we received from the security team told us to stay in our hotel. "We recommend that you do not go out in any public venue unless absolutely necessary," the email instructed.

So we stayed indoors. We attended the conference and related meetings, shuttling hurriedly between the hotel and conference center. The sentiment among our team was mixed. The days were sunny and warm. All of the Ethiopians we interacted with were kind and welcoming. Some in our group were unconcerned, sure that the warnings were overblown; others were terrified.

"Every Ethiopian I meet seems incredibly openhearted," I said to my colleague, complaining about being confined indoors.

"But that's not who we're worried about," my colleague reminded me, irritably. "It's the Somalis who are angry enough to gun us down. Don't you read the news?"

She was right. And still, I felt trapped. I kept thinking about my friend at church back at home, who had looked at me wistfully. "I've always wanted to go to Ethiopia. What an honor. Such a special opportunity."

And I wanted to seize that opportunity by slipping out for just a few hours to visit the nearby church. To acknowledge, in a small way, that I was walking on hallowed ground. To be a tiny part of it—even if only as a privileged tourist getting just a superficial glance at this ancient and mighty culture, brushing up against thousands of years of history.

My husband, David, was against it. He admonished me over Skype and email not to take any risks. Back at home, he talked to friends who agreed that, given the facts, it was unwise to venture out; he furiously relayed these opinions to me via text. In general, he worried that once I got an idea in my head, I wouldn't listen. He viewed me as a force of nature. Yet my instinct told me that it was okay, that I would be safe.

I was torn, not knowing what to do.

* * *

The dilemma I faced in Addis Ababa was just the latest in a series of difficult decisions I was navigating with David. Back at home, we were in the process of determining whether to become foster parents.

For the past seven years, beginning just a few months after our daughter, Lila, was born, I had been filled with a restless desire to have another baby. But David was sixteen years older than me. I knew when I met him and we decided to get married that the age difference would likely cause challenges. Yet I hadn't expected or been prepared for the intense divide that the "baby issue" would create. I hadn't anticipated how intensely I would want another child until Lila was born. In the weeks and months after her arrival, I fell in love with motherhood. David and I had been negotiating and debating the issue since then. We had been skillful and loving in our discussions, but there was no resolution between us.

A few months before I left for Ethiopia, David turned fifty. My stepson Soren, David's son from his first marriage, had started college that fall. David had been parenting for nearly twenty years, and he couldn't imagine starting all over, he explained. Yet I could not accept the alternative. I was in my mid-thirties, and I felt I had more mothering to do. With Soren launched, it was just the three of us. The house was too quiet. I wanted a bigger family.

We had talked off and on about the idea of becoming foster parents. After years of debate about whether to have another baby, the idea of fostering had emerged originally as an uneasy compromise between us. Yet in the past twelve months, as I had contemplated the possibility more seriously, the idea had started to become what felt like, for me, an authentic call.

Yet David remained unsure. He worried that there was no space in our lives to foster, that as busy professionals with full schedules at home and at work, we were already too overextended and exhausted to contemplate adding another major challenge in our lives. His admonishment over the choppy Skype connection in Addis Ababa echoed his unspoken feelings about the larger, more substantial discernment process that was underway. He worried that once I got an idea into my head, I wouldn't back down.

But the truth was, I felt confused about the fostering decision, too. On one hand, I could see all the ways that it was a crazy choice. It could add such a gigantic dollop of stress and discord to our lives that everything good we had built together—a happy home, a loving marriage, a well-adjusted daughter—could be thrown out of whack. This risk did not feel theoretical to me. Friends of ours had their lives turned upside down when a foster child they had lovingly accepted into their home turned on them and falsely accused them of abuse. The couple was forced into a year-long court battle with Social Services. Years after the incident had been resolved by a judge who rightly saw that our friends had been maligned, they still hadn't fully recovered from the pain. Their hurt was not just at the betrayal of the child's accusation, but also at how poorly the lawyers and their social workers had handled the situation.

Our friends' story was chilling, and the potential implications for our family were sobering. David is a self-employed psychologist in private practice. He works with families and kids in three different counties. If a foster child in our home falsely accused him of abuse, it wouldn't just be his personal reputation on the line. It would be his professional reputation—and his livelihood. The risks weighed heavily on both of us.

Yet despite the fears, there was also a whisper in my heart. I felt a promise that a child somewhere out there was waiting to come into our lives. I felt, perhaps irrationally, an urge to go for it.

Over the summer, the conversation about the decision had become so circular and exhausting for David and me that we had agreed to take a six-month break from all discussions about the issue. But now that hiatus was coming to an end. We had agreed to revisit the decision in January, so when I got back from this trip to Ethiopia, it would be time. This was the dilemma that loomed large in the back of my mind, forming a backdrop of uncertainty that added to the stress of travel, the long work hours, the grind of making dozens of minor daily decisions, the threat of terrorist attacks.

* * *

Back in Addis Ababa, gazing out of the window of my hotel at the busy street below, I remained uncertain whether to risk visiting the nearby church. I tried praying about the decision, but the result was confusing. I got both a *go* and *no-go* feeling in my prayers. I felt the Holy Spirit winding around me in tendrils, holding me in place. Yet at the same time, I felt an expectant *let's do this thing* sense from Jesus whenever I turned my attention his way.

Was I receiving contradictory calls on this issue from the different faces of the Trinity? Did that perception hold muster with any theologically sound conception of how God speaks to us? Or did it just reflect my own churning ambivalence about the decision?

So much of our prayer is fueled by imaginative power; how can one ever trust what happens in the mind? On the plane to Addis Ababa, the woman sitting next to me watched a new, extravagantly overblown zombie movie on her personal screen. I watched surreptitiously over her shoulder for twenty minutes. Closing my eyes during the rest of the flight, my thoughts became filled with explosive, violent, adrenaline-filled images. Clawing, desperate monsters and their blood-soaked victims. Fighting a morbid compulsion to open my eyes to see more, I contemplated how incredibly powerful the mind is. The imagination is a wild and often uncontrollable place. How, then, can we possibly trust that a prayerful discernment process that takes place within our minds will reveal any reliable truth about God's will for us? The Christian writer Simon Tugwell acknowledges that any religious experience "is always systematically ambiguous." We may feel magnificent as we kneel in prayer, "but that may be caused simply by a good dinner."

As Christians, we believe that God gave us free will. For me, the responsibility that comes with this feels overwhelming. Each question becomes weighty, like an overripe fruit on the vine. It can be exhausting to decide—over and over—what to do. What is the right path? What is the God-filled choice? What is God's will? How can I possibly discern it?

David, on the other hand, cannot comprehend how or why God would care about the specific choices we make. He has been a practicing Buddhist for over twenty-five years, and he believes that the point is to live virtuously, whatever our lot in life is. Why would God care, he asks, if we become a doctor or a lawyer or a bakery chef or a clerk at CVS or a foster parent? In any setting and in any role, we can practice compassion, patience, moral discipline, and love.

But as Christians, we believe in a God who counts the hairs on our head (Matthew 10:30). A God who is passionately invested in our rising up and our lying down (Psalm 139), our going out and our coming in (Psalm 121). A God who cares about the choices—big and small—that we make each day. This is not only because God cares deeply about us. It is because part of our job is to try to align our actions with God's vision and desires for us, especially—as we see in Jesus' journey to the cross—when this involves radical obedience and submission to God's will.

Every day in the hotel in Addis Ababa, as I contemplated the choices that lay before me, I read and re-read a single passage written by the theologian Henri Nouwen, who advises that contemplative prayer must be our cornerstone discipline. He writes, "Contemplative prayer keeps us home and safe, even when we are on the road, moving from place to place, and often surrounded by sounds of violence and war." He warns that, too easily, we can become rigidly fixated on our perceptions—and perhaps misperceptions—of God's will. The antidote is to remain "rooted in a deeply personal relationship with God," because otherwise, "before we know it, our sense of self is caught up in our opinion on a given subject."

I began experimenting with this practice in Addis Ababa. Sitting in the small hotel room—allowing the questions and decision-making to fall away—my mind grew calm.

In those moments, I felt a sense of Christ's presence. It reminded me of a glacier I visited once when I was traveling in New Zealand. Its hugeness was undeniable, its beauty breathtaking. And even though it appeared to be silent, frozen, and unmoving, the glacier was not static. It was moving at a pace, and in ways, we could not discern. It was a spring day when we visited, and even though the ice hung above us like a gigantic vertical river, we were warm on the ground below.

* * *

On the last day of our stay in Addis Ababa, a door opened up. A friend announced that, despite the risk, she was going to the local craft market, which was located next to the famous Trinity Church where the last Emperor of Ethiopia was buried. She didn't want to go out alone and needed a buddy. If I would accompany her, she would go to the church with me, and then we could take the taxi straight to the airport to catch our flight home. I hesitated, but there wasn't time for more deliberation. The next few hours were a flurry of activity as we packed, paid our bills, hailed a taxi, and navigated the market, where we were swarmed by dozens of men and women selling their wares.

But when we arrived at the church, a hush descended, and we were transported to another world.

A man outside stood at a stone pulpit and prayed in a steady chant in Aramaic. A dozen women sat silently, their heads and shoulders covered in pure white shawls. The tombstones of Ethiopia's fallen leaders crowded us on either side as we approached. Inside, the air was heavy with incense. We were the only visitors, and it was dark inside. Warm light streamed through the most vivid stained-glass windows I had ever seen.

As I stood to leave, the man who had guarded our shoes, which we had left at the door, reached out his hand for a tip. I placed a few small bills in his hand and then impulsively pulled him into a hug. He grinned at me and returned the embrace. I mumbled a few words of explanation, but he shook his head. He didn't speak English, but it seemed he understood. Brushing aside the tears on my cheek, I smiled and headed to the taxi that would take us to the airport.

A day and a half later, when I stepped out of the taxi in my driveway at home, David was standing on the front steps. His expression was difficult to read. I put my bags down, and he hugged me tightly. Sighing quietly, he pulled my heavy suitcase through the front door.

2
Bread Crumbs

By the time you're thirty, my grandfather used to say, waving his hands expansively, you should have a ten-year plan in place for your life. While decisions when you're younger don't have much bite, he would tell us, decisions made in your thirties and beyond do. Despite his advice, I've never had any ability to conceptualize a plan for my life. Instead, I feel like God leads me forward one step at a time, bread crumb by bread crumb. Never quite sure where the next crumb will appear, I always need to keep my eyes up, looking ahead, searching for the clue that will tell me which way the Spirit wants me to go. The result is that I pause often, uncertain, foot held aloft in mid-step, muscles trembling, as I wonder if I'm about to make a wrong turn.

Indecisiveness is not a quality that is typically admired in people. I've known leaders in organizations where I've worked and volunteered who have been criticized bitterly for their indecision on important issues; their lack of vision leaves their teams in a wake of confusion and insecurity.

Yet in the journey of life—and in particular, in a process of active discernment—is indecisiveness really such a terrible thing? In descriptions of his visits to monasteries across Europe, the travel writer Patrick Leigh Fermor describes the monks who came from every walk of life. They came from farms, universities, industry, the navy. The poor and the affluent. And during the period of preparation they all go through before taking their monastic vows, each is given multiple chances to back out. Fermor writes, "The possibility of withdrawal during the long years of novitiate is constantly kept before their eyes, with the result that all who take their final vows are deeply convinced of their vocation."

In that setting, indecision is welcomed as a critical part of formation. Wise mentors remind you that you can change course at any point during the preparation phase. And this gives you the opportunity to keep saying, "No, no, this feels right. *This* is for me." The process of forced self-reflection can lead to a ripening that results in a deep conviction of the rightness of the path to which one finally commits.

* * *

Was fostering the right choice for our family? One moment of clarity had come a month after I returned from Ethiopia. David and I were lying in bed, our legs entwined, his breathing even as he concentrated on his magazine article. I was flipping through a book, skimming over random passages every few pages—until my eyes rested on words that seemed to sear through me.

Isn't it strange how a book can speak to you? More than that, how God can speak to us through the written word, in myriad formats and styles? The well-known writer Richard Foster describes how astonished he always is that "God can take something so inadequate, so imperfect, so foolish as words on paper and use them to transform lives."

Just that week, I had tried, imperfectly, to communicate my truth through the written word. I had given David a letter—hoping to get his attention and make him really think about the question I wanted to pose. "Please," I pleaded with him, in the note I gave him, "tell me if you're really open to pursuing this fostering thing. If not, let me know now. I can't keep obsessing and pouring emotional energy into this issue." He read the letter. That night, he told me he was willing to do it. He knew how important the possibility of fostering was to me, and after reflecting about the idea for a long time, he decided he was up for it.

But, he said, he questioned my motivation. He was skeptical about my true agenda. He feared that my secret desire was to adopt a child.

"If we're going to do this, you have to hear me," David

said. "I'm willing to foster, but I'm just not up for the life-long commitment of raising another child. I'm just not up for it. This is why I don't want to have another baby. It is one thing to do something for six or twelve months. We can survive anything for a year. Adoption is a totally different level of commitment." He looked at me steadily. "Can we agree that we'll only foster? Can you live with that?"

"Yes, I think so. I really do." I nodded slowly. We had talked about this before, and I had given it a lot of thought. "I understand your position. If you're willing to do this with me, I will commit to only fostering."

But after the conversation, I kept mulling over the question, wondering if I was being honest with myself. Could I really commit to only foster and not adopt? What if we fell in love with a child and he or she needed a place to stay permanently? Could I let the child go? Would I have the strength to do that?

Until that evening in bed, lying beside David as he read his magazine article, I was unsure. Then the words in the book I was reading by Caryll Houselander—a popular twentieth century writer, artist, and mystic— jumped out at me. She wrote, "It is part of God's plan for us that Christ shall come to us in everyone. He may come as a little child, making enormous demands, giving enormous consolation. He may come as a stranger, so that we must give the hospitality to a stranger that we should like to give to Christ.... If we see everyone in our life as 'another Christ,' as a matter of sheer logic, we shall accept whatever they bring us, in the way of joy or sorrow or responsibility."

I felt it then. Christ would come to us, to our family, in a myriad of forms. As the child. As the stranger. This would be our adventure. Our adventure with God. Whatever joy or sorrow or responsibility—or loss—came with it.

Houselander went on to say that once we learn to see Christ in everyone, we will never "again miss a joy that should have been ours through another person because we dared not give ourselves to it bravely."

It was time to give myself to it bravely.

* * *

The truth is, I'm not brave. That weekend, I had to press the go button, literally. I had to email my RSVP to the social worker for the foster care class. In the last twenty-four hours before the deadline for responding, it was like I was going through the final phases of a terrible detox, with doubt and fear oozing out of my pores. I was sweaty and weepy. It felt as though a powerful toxin was being flushed out of my system. Perhaps it was the illusion that I was in control. God wanted me to do this, I could feel it. I could feel it like a drill, pushing through all of the rock until it reached the precious ore at the center of things. All of the alternative paths I could possibly take were pushed aside by its power. God did not want me to start a business or volunteer at a food bank or join an important new committee at church or do a million other things. God wanted me to do this one strange, surprising, messy, simple, unglamorous thing.

I sent the email with our RSVP. We'd be there on Thursday for the class.

And then there was a lightness. In the days that followed, I felt like I had gotten a chiropractic adjustment. Like something subtle yet profound had clicked into place. I wasn't just moving forward—I was on the path. On *my* path.

* * *

On the first night of the mandatory ten-week course for prospective foster parents, we were given the opportunity to back out. "Some of you won't be coming back after the first or second or third session. That's fine. There's no shame in that," the social worker said, in the first few minutes of her opening remarks. "This is a partnership. You're figuring out if it's a match for you, and at the same time, we're figuring out if you'll be a fit." Her clipped words were matter-of-fact, but not unkind. "If you don't come back, please just return the manual we've given you so that we can reuse it."

Our eyes bugged at the two-hundred-page binder in front of us on the table. The prospect of wading through the packet of materials seemed like it alone would scare off half the group.

There were twenty-four of us. The group defied all of my stereotypes, beginning with the size of the class. I figured it would just be me and David, and at most, one or two other couples. I imagined that they would mostly be people who had gotten stuck with nephews or grandchildren—children who had been taken from their parents and then placed by social services with the nearest living relative who was willing to take them. Or, I guessed, the class would be filled with people who were poor and who planned to use the stipend provided for food and clothes for foster children, as supplementary income. I imagined sitting in a dark room, in small, uncomfortable chairs, listening to a disengaged social worker drone on about rules, regulations, and a litany of pitfalls to avoid, while the participants answered her questions with monosyllabic responses.

Yet the class was made up of a dynamic group. With plates of pizza balanced on the sodas that the instructor offered us as we walked in, David and I sat at a narrow table near the front of the room. Next to us was Christine—a tall, African-American woman in a stylish suit, her ankles tucked beneath the table, beside a handsome leather briefcase. Flashing a smile as we shook hands and greeted each other, she mentioned she had two adult children and was a senior finance officer at the local university. As we settled in, we began with brief introductions around the circle. There were young professionals, grandparents, a single mother, a lesbian couple, a truck driver and his wife, who homeschooled their three teenagers. The social worker nodded. She wanted us to get to know each other. We were going to become like a family over the next three months, she explained. We were told to pair up with someone in the group and talk about our reasons for being there.

My partner, Sheila, was a nurse. She lived off the highway in a rural area, with her husband, two donkeys, and a dozen guinea hens. Why was she taking the class? Sheila explained that she'd read an article in the newspaper about a girl whose parents had been killed in a car wreck. The girl had no living relatives. The story had been so compelling that Sheila had called the girl's pastor, who was mentioned in the news story, and offered to adopt the girl then and there. She learned that the girl had gone to live with someone in the church, but the experience prompted Sheila to call social services to learn more about the process, and she'd heard about this class. Listening to her story, I tried to hide my skepticism. I knew enough to recognize that fostering or adopting through social services is not like scooping up Little Orphan Annie, tragically and suddenly abandoned. These were kids who were abused and neglected—often routinely so, over years. Did Sheila know what she was getting into? Did she have what it took? Was she someone who would drop out after the first class? Or after the second or third?

She looked at me with a friendly, open face. "Why are you taking the class? How do you know fostering is right for your family?"

There was the question again. I was like the novitiate, in a long process of formation, in another moment of forced self-reflection.

"I've been hungry for another child in my life for years,"

I replied stiffly, trying to simplify seven years of heartache into a sound bite.

* * *

Back in the large group, we continued around the room with our introductions. One of the women, Julie, had stylish glasses and wavy hair tucked around her ears. She smiled broadly. "Why am I here? I vividly remember asking my mother, when I was a little girl, 'Why do people have babies when so many kids in the world need families?' I continue to ask myself that question every day. That's why I'm here." She sat, still smiling. For her, it was as simple as that.

After the introductions, we did another exercise called "Imagine If." The social worker asked if David and I would be willing to volunteer for the activity. In front of the group, she asked us to talk about Soren and Lila. She asked us to describe how we would feel if our kids were suddenly taken away from us. The exercise was meant to help the group empathize with the biological parents of the children in foster care. Even if they did monstrous things, the ordeal of having their kids taken away was traumatic.

As the class ended that night, the social worker again acknowledged that some of us might not be coming back the next week. "But Kate and David, you have to return." She smiled at us.

Startled, I looked at David. Why had she singled us out?

"It's because the last few times we did that exercise,

"Imagine If," in this class, the volunteers we selected didn't return the next week. We can't have it turn into a pattern." The social worker smiled at us, and the class laughed. We cleared our pizza plates and said our goodbyes.

As I headed out to the parking lot, the cold air hit my face. I grinned. I'd loved it. I loved the class, the people. I was hooked. We'd definitely be back.

3

sliver

ON THE SECOND MEETING of the class, the size of the group had shrunk by a third. Sheila the nurse was gone. The truck driver and his homeschooling wife were gone. Christine was still there, and I sat beside her with a grateful smile. I was glad we were in this together—at least for now.

I was glad for all the familiar faces. The lesbian couple, Anna and Sylvie, were back. Jane and Simon, a sweet couple who owned a restaurant downtown, were there. Jane's face perpetually seemed to have the appearance of a startled rabbit, eyes wide and searching. I had wondered if she would return. Stewart, a heavyset man in his fifties, who had asked a series of perceptive questions the week before, cracked a few jokes as the group settled in. We all laughed and chatted with our neighbors. It was like we were old friends.

But as the evening progressed, the anxiety level in the group creeped up palpably. We reviewed profiles of kids in the system. Jaycee, Brian, Carla—each situation more horrible than the one before. Stewart started shifting in his seat. Jane, with her rabbit eyes, began blinking rapidly. My own heart rate accelerating, I dropped my eyes and started flipping through the pages of my manual, nervously. Fetal alcohol syndrome, attachment disorders, medically fragile children. The material on the pages did nothing to calm me. I kept flipping. Maybe the next chapter would have something more reassuring and uplifting, like, *What to do when you get placed with a well-adjusted child who just can't seem to stop thanking you for all the ways you've touched their life.*

David was quiet. Aside from the social workers, he was the only one in the room who knew what we were getting ourselves into. As part of his psychology practice, he conducts forensic evaluations for the courts. He assesses sex offenders, advising whether treatment might help, and predicting the likelihood that they will reoffend. He carries out parenting evaluations to assess the mental health needs and competency of parents who have been neglectful. And he provides therapy to kids who have been abused and are in the system. After a few years of listening to clients' stories over the dinner table, I had to ask him to stop sharing the details. It was traumatizing me. I couldn't stop imagining the face of the seventeen-year-old kid whose father had beat him until he was almost uncon-scious when he'd been caught fondling his younger sister. The father had dragged him to the police station until the kid confessed under oath. The judge—eager to be seen as tough on crime—had tried the seventeen-year-old as an adult, and he'd gotten fifteen years in jail. David said the kid had a round, soft face, and blinked with tears in his eyes when he was in David's office for the evaluation. The kid was a victim of sexual abuse himself.

David was lying low in the foster care class. He didn't want anyone to know he was an expert, concerned that the social workers would target our family to receive their toughest cases.

"It seems like it will be a therapeutic project," David said, flatly, over dinner the next night when I asked him how he thought the class was going. "I know how to do therapy. I'm not sure I particularly want to do it in this context. But I know how to."

I became animated. "You don't have to see it like that, you know. Sure, it won't be the same as parenting our own kids. But you don't have to be cold and clinical about it. It will be in our home. It won't be like doing therapy. It has the possibility of being something different, something full of love." I paused, the last sentence coming out qui-etly. "Something that could even be transformative for *us*."

David shrugged noncommittally.

I launched into my typical defensive monologue. "David, I just feel like this is a calling. I just feel it. Don't you understand?"

"Yes, I do. But it's just that I'm not on this conference line. They didn't dial me in on this one. This is your call, not mine." His words came out quietly, but firmly.

"So why are you going along and doing this?" My breath came out sharply.

"For you. It's your dream. I'm doing it so that you can scratch the itch and get this thing you want so badly."

I bristled. This is not what I wanted to hear. Everything David and I had ever done together—getting married, parenting Soren, having Lila, building an addition on our house, even me going to graduate school—had been a joint endeavor of the heart. Something that we both bought into equally, as a team. I was worried that this might be different. That I was forcing David to do something he wasn't convinced was good for him or our family. All of my alarm bells were going off.

I retreated from the conversation. On one hand, I was touched. Awed, even. No one had ever loved me enough to do something like this before. Sure, my parents had made ordinary sacrifices, but no one had ever put their desires on the back burner and told me that my dream came first. It was a lesson for me about love. At the same time, I didn't know if I could trust it. Would operating this way cause resentment to simmer and eventually boil over? David's position seemed generous on one hand, but from his tone, I sensed the tension beneath the words. There didn't seem to be any joy, only resignation.

And even if David didn't end up resenting the decision, I wasn't sure how to respond to his willingness to sacrifice his own needs to meet mine. I kept thinking about the time our neighbors had squirrels invade their attic. Their solution was to put a tub of water out, with a thin layer of bird seed floating on top. The squirrels dove in, thinking the food was on firm footing, only to fall through to the water below. Soon, the neighbors had a bucket full of drowned squirrels. In my case, I didn't know whether to trust the sacrificial love David was offering. I didn't know if I was on firm footing, or if it would turn out to be a dangerous illusion.

Perhaps, the fact that I couldn't stop thinking about drowned squirrels meant I didn't understand the true nature of sacrifice or love.

* * *

David had always been the sure and steady one when it came to making big decisions. When we had been dating for only a few months, he blurted out, "I want to marry you," his eyes shining with the excitement at our new-found love.

"Stop!" I'd covered my ears. "You can't say that. It's too soon."

From then on, to tease me, he would say, "I want to m-m-m-m…," drawing out the word, as I'd squawk. As a joke, he would change the ending of the sentence at the last moment, "I want to m-m-monkey you."

Silly and in love, we decided we'd get "monkeyed" first before we got married, agreeing that it was a solemn and lifelong commitment. I found two stuffed animal monkeys in a toy store and presented them to him. Six months later, when he proposed for real in a field full of daisies, I was still skittish. I asked whether being "engaged" could mean that we were "deeply engaged," but not necessarily that we were going to get married. He looked at me incredulously. "No, I'm not going to tell everyone that we're *deeply engaged*. If we're engaged, we're getting married. If we're not, we're not."

I backed down and said yes. We could get married.

And as soon as the decision was made, I was all in. My lifelong pattern is to be scared and noncommittal at first. But once I commit, I'm like a snapping turtle with the strongest jaws. I never let go. Ten years after marrying David, I considered it one of the best decisions I had ever made.

So it was a new and uncomfortable position for me to be the one driving us forward into a big commitment. For the first time, I was the one pushing him into something that he was doing only reluctantly. This role reversal seemed fraught with emotional uncertainty and risk. In this context, accepting his sacrifice felt like a vulnerable and dangerous thing.

I knew that accepting another's tremendous, life-altering sacrifice is an important part of the Christian story, since we are all invited to accept the ultimate sacrifice that Jesus made for us. But I remained a neophyte and didn't fully understand what it was all about. That week at church, I approached the altar rail for communion. *What is sacrifice?* I called out to Jesus, silently, in my prayers. How can I understand the sacrifice you made? What does that word even *mean*?

I held my hands out to receive the Eucharist offering. My church distributes delicious homemade bread for communion, and we usually each get a sizable chunk. But that day, for whatever reason, only a minuscule triangle was placed into my hand. It was a perfect tiny sliver.

In that moment, I realized how inept I am at loving people. It's all about the experience of pleasure for me. Kissing my daughter's unbearably soft skin fills me with good feelings. What if she wasn't so cute, so appealing, so healthy, so well-adjusted? If I'm being honest with myself, would I love her just a sliver less? Likewise, my marriage with David was often about negotiating to get what I wanted, instead of asking myself if and how I could make sacrifices for him or our relationship.

But then, as I felt the tiny piece of bread in my mouth, the insight came to me like a gift. Truly, love and sacrifice are synonyms. Christ's sacrifice was love. And he is in me. Through the Eucharist, he continues to enact his sacrificial love through our relationship. And of course, we're all inept when it comes to sacrificial love. That's why we need Christ so badly. He does it in us and for us. In my relationship with David, I could make and accept sacrifices, and rely on God to help navigate the challenges and vulnerability involved.

* * *

Later that week, at the end of the third session of the

foster care class, the social worker said something that gave me more pause than all of her warnings about the emotional baggage and disturbed behavior we were likely to see in our foster children. She said, "If you're going to become foster parents, you should do it to help the kids, not for yourself."

I grew still. Again, if I was being honest with myself, I knew I was there—in the class, and engaged in the process—for a slew of selfish reasons. I was trying to address an unsatisfied hunger that lurked as an ever-present shadow in my life. I was hoping for meaning, for satisfaction, for connection. Deep down, I knew I wasn't there because I wanted to help somebody who was in a difficult situation. I was in it for me.

I thought back to my insight at the communion rail. Do we ever truly do anything selflessly, at least at the outset? What biological parents' motivations are altruistic before their baby is born? Would a pregnant woman bat heavy eyelashes and say, "I didn't get pregnant for myself. I just did it because I wanted to help an unborn child." Maybe a few, but not most parents I know. The people I know, including myself, jumped into parenting because we thought it would bring meaning to our lives, or that it would be fun, or because we couldn't imagine life without the experience of parenting, or because we thought we could do a pretty good job at it, or because we wanted to leave our mark and a legacy in the world.

But of course, once the baby arrives, it becomes one selfless moment after another. By necessity, we're absorbed with wiping the poop, cleaning the spit-up, sacrificing sleep and sanity to nurture, care for, and protect. We stay awake at night, worrying and wondering about our kids' well-being. We risk advancement and reputation at work when we try to be at both the school event and an important meeting with colleagues on the same afternoon. We attempt to respond patiently when we're asked by the toddler, for the eighty-sixth time that day, "Why? Why do I have to do it? Why does it work that way? Why, why, why?"

Before the child comes, we only have the tiniest sliver of understanding of the sacrifice involved. We don't know or understand how parenting will rob us of our self-absorbed, self-directed, self-entitled ways, and provide us instead with something far bigger and more precious: the opportunity to be our best, most loving selves.

I could only hope that my selfishness would be replaced by that kind of love if and when we became foster parents.

In her journal, Flannery O'Connor wrote, "Dear God, you are the slim crescent of a moon that I can see, and myself is the earth's shadow that keeps me from seeing all the moon....I do not know you, God, because I am in the way. Please help me to push myself aside."

Maybe it's enough to only see the sliver of the moon at the beginning. Perhaps it's enough, at the outset, to have only a hint of the gigantic love that is out there and that lies within us, full of potential. As we learn to step aside and get out of our own way, we experience more and more our capacity to love selflessly. Perhaps this was why

David was willing to take the plunge. He didn't want to end up like a drowned squirrel any more than I did. But he was willing to trust that the sliver of sacrificial love he felt in his heart would grow and grow, until it eclipsed the reluctance and uncertainty so the full moon could shine and penetrate the dark.

4

A Disney Lent

"For the love of God, what are you going to give up?" My mother blurted out the question like it had been pent up inside her for a while.

It was the same question family and friends kept asking me, over and over, as I discussed the possibility of becoming a foster parent. People asked it in different ways, most treading lightly with gentle, sideways questions, presumably to avoid triggering a defensive response in me.

My mother's version was the most blunt. "Your life is so full already. What are you going to give up to make all of this work?"

This question, which had become a constant refrain, felt like the central dilemma. It was the same question I kept asking myself. The truth was, I didn't want to give up anything in my life. I didn't want to jeopardize a career that had, over the past few years, finally started to gain a momentum of its own. I didn't want to give up time with David or Lila. I didn't want to cut out the time I devoted to my daily prayer practice or to my writing. At the same time, I knew I couldn't do it all. I had learned—from long, hard experience—that I easily became anxious and overwrought if I tried to do too much. My life felt like a constant high-wire balancing act. Doing too little left me feeling bored and impotent; doing too much, I quickly became frazzled. I am always trying to find and walk along the elusive path between the two extremes.

My mother's question coincided with the beginning of Lent. A time when we're called to give something up or to take on a new commitment, Lent is viewed as a season of preparation. As we move toward Good Friday and Easter, the practices of self-examination, repentance, fasting, and self-denial allow us to look inward and identify the blockages that are keeping us from getting closer to God.

It turned out that that year, Disney World was my best and most powerful Lenten teacher. Disney taught me a lesson that helped save me from myself.

* * *

Disney World is a strange place to visit at any time of the year, and it is an especially strange place to go during Lent. But that year, Lila's spring break was scheduled for a few weeks before Easter, so that's when we went. Before the family trip, I discovered that when you tell others that you are going to Disney World, there are two kinds of people: Those who suck in their breath, their eyes becoming unfocused as they gaze off over your shoulder, murmuring reverentially about how lucky you are. Then there are those who stare at you blankly—clearly incredulous that anyone would want to spend their precious time and money visiting the one place on earth that would make them want to jump off a cliff.

Before we left, I fell into the second category. We were going because a few years before, my father had declared that it was his dream to go to Disney World with his only grandchild. You could tell this was a Dream with a capital "D" by the tone in his voice; I didn't ever want to be the person who stood in the way of that kind of dream. Yet I remained unenthusiastic about the trip. My daughter is a textbook introvert, and I worried that my dad's expectations, my daughter's energy level, and the overblown Disney spectacle would be a disastrous combination.

Earlier that month, during the first week of Lent, I had adopted a personalized ritual intended to help me let go of things that were holding me back spiritually, and in my life in general. I put a beautiful purple bowl out in the middle of my kitchen table. Every time a fear or insecurity or petty jealousy emerged that seemed to get in the way of my relationship with God or my neighbor, I wrote the unruly thought down on a piece of paper and dropped it into the bowl. I described the items on the paper as my "neurotic mental junk"—or my NMJ, as I started calling them. In my prayers, Jesus lay in the middle of that bowl, stretching it out like it was still on the potter's wheel so the walls became thinner and the vessel was able to hold more and more.

Every Friday evening, as Lent progressed, I lit a fire in the bowl and burned the pieces of paper. Each week, when they were cool enough to touch, I sifted my fingers through the growing mound of ashes. Although the pile kept getting bigger, there was almost nothing substantial left. The ashes were as light as the softest silk.

The day before we left for Disney World, I burned some more slips of paper with my NMJ written them. On top of the stack, I placed my biggest and most stubborn misconception. I wrote, "I can do it all." When I lit the paper on fire, a strange thing happened. The paper burned, but it retained its exact size and shape; it had become a perfect square of ash, without even a curl in the corner. Even more strange was that although the fire had shot through the paper, I could still read the imprint of my lettering. The statement, "I can do it all," stared up at me, the ink faded to a reddish purple.

I poured water on top of the ash until the paper was soggy and the words illegible. But I had gotten the message. I wasn't ready to give up this NMJ quite yet. I might have burned it symbolically, but I was still carrying it around with me.

The next morning, when we arrived in Orlando, I was shocked by the size of the resort. Disney World spans the same number of square miles as two Manhattans, I read on my phone as we drove in from the airport. The statistics were staggering. According to the Fun Facts website, every year, two million pounds of ketchup are consumed, three million chocolate covered Mickey Mouse ice cream bars are eaten, and over a million firework shells are fired. Every day, more than thirty thousand character costumes require dry cleaning; Mickey alone appears in nearly three hundred costumes at various locations. *This is a place of utter excess*, I thought. People come here to live out the fantasy that wishing on a star will make all your dreams come true, despite the fine print that warns it will require a second mortgage on your house.

Yet as soon as we arrived at the Magic Kingdom that afternoon, my judgements and worries dissipated. Lila loved it, my father was relaxed, the lines for the rides weren't outrageous. But more than that, I immediately started having fun. I was totally into it. I wanted to do everything—try every ride, meet every character, sing along with every classic childhood song. It was like being swept up in the biggest pep rally of the year, right before the high school homecoming game, when no matter how much snobby distaste you try to maintain for the garish display of all things American, you find yourself screaming as loudly as the most enthusiastic cheerleader.

I also realized that if you try to do it all, you end up cranky, exhausted, sick to your stomach, and broke, within a few days.

My family's Disney World mantra became, *We can't do it all. We just can't make it to the Princess Pavilion Parade at 11:10, in front of Cinderella's castle, and also make it to*

Splash Mountain and the Barnstormer roller coaster for a second ride. Disney also became a reminder that I'm part of an ecosystem of a family, and as such, we're bound to each other as a team. Personally, I could have spent four more hours running around Hollywood Studios. I wanted to see Indiana Jones narrowly avoid being crushed by a gigantic boulder, and I wanted to watch the Muppets in 3D, but my dad was drooping and Lila had gotten a sunburn. Maybe I could have done more, but as a family, we couldn't do it all.

I learned the lesson while I was at Disney, but within the first week of returning home, I almost forgot it. A few days after our vacation, a temptation of excess was placed in front of me at work that held more allure than the most enticing Disney attraction. I was invited to apply for a prestigious short-term grant to work on an issue I cared about deeply. The catch was that the project would require a herculean list of tasks to be completed on an impossible six-month timeline. It was a rare professional opportunity that, realistically, might not ever come along again. Yet if we applied and got the grant, I knew I would be at risk of a nervous breakdown if I tried to deliver what the funder wanted. Plus, I kept trying to remind myself that the plan had been to scale back at work so I could focus on becoming a foster parent.

But then I thought, maybe I could squeeze in one more thing. Rationally, I knew I couldn't do it all, but I wanted to try. The temptation was strong to keep pushing the limits.

During the last few days of Lent, I contemplated the purple bowl, which had held all of my NMJ over the previous weeks. I had burned all the remaining slips of paper, poured water onto the fire, and dumped the ashy mess into the backyard garden. After scooping out every remaining scrap of debris with my fingers, the bowl was clean. I thought back to the slip of paper that had burned yet retained its shape and the words written on it. Could I do it all?

In that moment, looking at the empty bowl in front of me, I realized that I was asking the wrong question.

I hear the refrain, "I'm so busy," from everyone in my life—friends, coworkers, even church friends who are retired. We seem to measure our lives by the barometer of whether we're doing too much. But what if there is a different metric by which we should evaluate our lives? The question is not whether I can do it all, or how full my calendar should be, or whether I can ever achieve the right balance of busyness and downtime. The real question is to what degree can I empty my heart to make space for God.

In those months of preparation—as we continued with the foster care class—I didn't know whether God wanted me to invest more energy into my career, or whether God wanted me to scale back at work and go inward with my family to take on a new challenge of fostering. There were so many unknowns. I didn't know if we'd get the new grant even if we applied, or what would happen if we decided to pass on the funding opportunity. I didn't know when Social Services would call us with an invitation to take a foster placement, or if something else unexpected would happen that would change the equation of my life. In the face of all the uncertainty, I realized that I just needed to focus on keeping my heart and mind free of junk so I would be ready to respond whenever and however God called me to serve. While I couldn't do it all, I could try to keep my bowl as empty as possible so God could fill me up as God saw fit.

Bernard of Clairvaux writes, "If then you are wise, you will show yourself rather as a reservoir than as a canal. For a canal spreads abroad water as it receives it, but a reservoir waits until it is filled before overflowing, and thus communicates, without loss to itself, its superabundant waters." As Lent came to an end, I knew that the task ahead was to keep allowing my NMJ to burn up in Jesus' cleansing fire. Once it had been reduced to ash, my hope was that his superabundant waters would fill me up and overflow.

PART TWO

The Placement

5
Delays

DAVID AND I COMPLETED the foster care training class.
Of the original twenty-four people who had started, six
of us graduated. But even after the weekly meetings were
done, the process was not complete. The social worker
conducted a series of lengthy home visits, first interview-
ing us one-on-one, and then together. She made notes
in her binder while we talked, and I wondered what she
was writing down. Friends had to write letters of recommendation for us, and we were required to go to the
doctor for physicals. Even Soren, who was at college most
of the year, was required to go through these steps. They
ran blood tests on each of us, testing for tuberculosis and
other infectious diseases. David, Soren, and I went to the
sheriff's office for fingerprinting; the background checks

came back clear. The fire department did an inspection of our house. To pass, we were required to hang up a fire extinguisher in the hallway, and an emergency exit plan in the kitchen.

Five days later, the certificate arrived in the mail. We were licensed foster parents.

And then we waited. Nothing happened. Weeks passed. We realized that it could take a while, given that our criteria for the type of placement we would accept was narrow. We would only take a child under age five because we wanted a substantial age gap with Lila to help her feel secure and to keep her safe from any abuse. We would only accept one child at a time. Most kids in foster care are placed with at least one brother or sister; Social Services does everything they can to keep siblings together.

Social Services called us a few times that fall. The first time, just after Labor Day, they asked if we'd take two brothers, four and six years old. Stacey, the social worker, knew we had said during the interviews that we didn't want a sibling pair, but she explained in a warm voice that she was just calling to double-check. Three weeks later, another call, this time for a nine-month-old baby girl and her two-year-old sister. Again, Stacey just wanted to check to see if we were interested. Both times, I hesitated, but I knew two would be too much. Fitting one child into our lives would already be pushing it with everything we were juggling. "I'm sorry," I told Stacey, on the phone. "But we just can't."

Then, no more calls. They seemed to have gotten the

message and had taken us off the sibling-pair placement list. Every day, I wondered if we would get a call. I would be in a meeting or at the grocery store and stare down at my phone. When would they contact us again? If they called now, would we say yes? If we said yes, would that mean a child could be placed with us that same day?

I was on edge all the time. But still, nothing. Then one afternoon in November, I was getting ready for a week-long work trip to Mexico City. My flight left at 5 a.m. the next day. I folded clothes and put them in my suitcase while I ran through lists in my mind. PowerPoint slides were on the USB stick, handouts for the training in the yellow folder, articles in my carry-on to read on the plane, babysitter for Lila confirmed for Tuesday afternoon, juice boxes and twelve bags of pretzels on the counter, ready for David to take to soccer practice. The phone rang. It was Stacey. "We have an eighteen-month-old boy who needs a placement. Could you take him this afternoon?"

I looked at the black roller bag on my bed. My passport and my boarding pass—which I had just printed out—were on the bedside table.

I paused for a moment, but I knew what my answer would be. "I'm so sorry. I just can't. I'm leaving at the crack of dawn for a work trip. I couldn't leave David here alone to manage such a huge transition."

"No problem," Stacey said, cheerfully. "You're on our list. We'll keep calling."

* * *

But they didn't call again. It was as though everything

had stopped. The sense of God-given clarity and purpose dwindled. Everything related to fostering seemed to go radio silent. I wasn't sure if we had been blacklisted by Social Services because our criteria was too narrow or because we'd turned down the placements when they had called.

And then the snow came. North Carolina gets a dusting of snow every other year or so. But that winter, it was a deluge; we got ten inches one night, and then six more the next day. Lila made a sled out of a flimsy plastic garden tray she found in our shed. Five-foot-tall snowmen appeared in almost every yard. Unaccustomed to the weight of snow and ice, tree branches were down everywhere. Half the homes in our small town were without power.

And of course, there was no school. North Carolina schools close with even the threat of possible inclement weather. With snow piled up everywhere and the roads impassable, there was no question. But then the snow started to melt. The roads opened up. Yet the schools stayed closed. "There's still a threat of ice," the television told us. "Unsafe road conditions." David and I did our best to juggle.

The day that Lila finally returned to school, I felt like an avalanche hit me. It was my first full day in the office in ten days, and there was a frenzy of catch-up: meetings that had been rescheduled, missed emails to read through, a new funding opportunity to evaluate.

At four o'clock, David called.

"I can't talk," I said, irritably. "There's leftovers in the fridge for dinner if you want to eat before I get there."

"Stacey just called," David said. "They have a baby that needs a placement. A five-month-old boy with a broken arm."

I couldn't breathe. My eyes filled with tears. I looked at my calendar. We were scheduled to complete a mid-project review that week; we had over twenty-five hours of team meetings planned. I told David I would call him back.

"Hurry," he said. "The social worker's waiting for our decision. Whoever takes the baby will have to spend tomorrow in the hospital with him."

I sat there. How could I drop everything? Snowpocalypse—as we had termed it—had just ended. It would take a week to catch up. My team was counting on me to participate in the project review. There was no space in my brain to ask God for help or to listen to what God might have to say about this. I just kept saying over and over, to myself, "I can't do it. I just can't do it. I can't." I put my head down. "I can't drop everything and take a baby with a broken arm tomorrow. Maybe if I had a couple of weeks—even a few days—to plan. But this is too much. I can't, I can't, I can't." The words thrummed in me as I headed for my car.

I called David, and then Stacey, on my way home. "I'm so sorry. I'm so embarrassed. If you'd even called a week later, it would be different, but things are so crazy. The snow…I'm so behind. …"

"No worries at all." Stacey's voice was reassuring. "A baby will be easy to place. I just wanted to give your family the opportunity. Don't worry."

But all I could do was worry. I worried about the baby. What happened to him? How did he end up with a broken arm? Would he be okay? Was it selfish and wrong to say no to the placement? I also worried that, in a bigger sense, I was letting God down, that I was giving up on a long-fought-for dream of fostering.

But, at the same time, I was also immensely relieved.

I called a friend that night, hoping she could provide some cosmic-level advice. I wanted to process this glacier of an event that had drifted into my life and smashed my evenings to bits.

"Don't worry," she said, echoing the social worker's words. "Fostering will happen when the time is right."

When the time is right? Her words reminded me of the concept of *kairos*, a Greek word used in the New Testament, which means the right or opportune moment for action. *Kairos*—which differs from *chronos*, or ordinary time—reflects God's agenda and timeline, not ours. The theologian Paul Tillich wrote extensively about *kairos*; in the New Testament the word is meant to "reveal the maturity of time in which the Kingdom of god may manifest itself." A priest I know once explained to me that at the beginning of church, she always removes her watch. For her, this is a reminder that during the Eucharist, she's on God's time, not her own.

That evening, as I questioned my decision about the

placement we'd been offered, I recognized that part of having faith is waiting to act until the time is right in God's eyes. It means waiting for the *kairos* moment to emerge.

* * *

Stacey called again on the Friday before the Fourth of July. Nearly a year had passed since we'd gotten our foster care license in the mail.

"We have a two-and-half year old girl," Stacey said. "She needs a placement this evening. Can you take her?"

I was sitting at my desk at work. There were twenty unread emails in my inbox, a two-page to-do list lying on my desk. But it was a long weekend. The work would wait. My parents were arriving for a visit that afternoon. I had a sudden fluttery, confident feeling in my throat. This was it. This was the one. I didn't pause.

I called David. "I think we should say yes."

"Okay, if you think it's right, I'm up for it," he replied.

I called Stacey back.

Alyana arrived that evening at seven o'clock. We watched her come up the driveway, holding the social worker's hand. When she arrived, we had several toys laid out on the small rug in front of our fireplace. We all crouched together, looking at the magnet puzzle that had been a favorite of Lila's years before. Lila stood behind David at first, observing silently, then joined us on the carpet, helping Alyana to manipulate the pieces into place. My parents hung back in the den, watching the scene through the doorway, from the couch.

Alyana had wavy, sandy blond hair and deep brown eyes that stared up into mine. I noticed that her eyelashes were so long they curled up far beyond the top of her lids, almost touching her eyebrows.

In the subsequent hours, days, and weeks, I would fall in love with this girl. We imprinted on each other like a mother and baby duck. She became a child of our hearts. She started calling us Mommy and Daddy within the first forty-eight hours, and, even though we tried to discourage her use of the terms, she never stopped. She was a terrible listener, blatantly mischievous. She aggravated us, exhausted us, challenged us. She would sometimes hit and bite kids at daycare. She was constantly on the go, with the attention span of a gnat, restlessly needing new activities, and requiring constant supervision. But she was funny, affectionate, inquisitive, and remarkably well-adjusted for a kid in "the system." She slept and ate well. She was so relentlessly joyful and extroverted that at times we joked that she had an "exuberance disorder." She was as smart as any toddler I'd ever met. We all adored her. One day, after she had been with us six months, she threw her arms up in the air at dinner and cried, "I love this family!" She became my sweetheart, David's little buddy, a sister to Lila. She became ours.

She stayed with us exactly nine months. Time enough for love to gestate into something fully formed. Then she left.

And I let her go.

6

Main Street

IT IS A STRANGE THING to be married to a psychologist in a small college town. While interacting with strangers, I never know if I'm talking to one of David's clients. One time, I was leaning back in the chair at the hair salon, getting my hair washed before a cut. The stylist let the warm water soak my scalp, and then after massaging me behind the ears, rinsed the suds away. My eyes were half-closed.

"Your husband is great," the stylist said, while she wrung out my hair.

"What?" My eyes snapped open.

I had never met this woman before; a friend had referred me to the salon, and it was my first time going there.

"Oh, he's been my therapist for three years. He's really great. Super wise. He's so calm. And funny, too." She put a towel around my shoulders. "Okay, follow me to the chair."

I followed slowly, unnerved. This woman thought my husband was great? They'd had a three-year-long, intimate relationship with one another? I had never heard about her or seen her before?

"Okay, so what do you want to do with your hair today?" She looked at me expectantly, pushing my hair forward over my ears.

"Um, I was thinking about cutting it to just above my shoulders."

The woman didn't mention David again. The haircut turned out well, but I never went back to that salon.

Or there was the time we bumped into a couple at the grocery store. My husband stopped to chat, and I assumed they were his clients. I made myself scarce to honor their confidentiality, staying at a respectable distance and staring for an overly long time at a poster in the glassed-in bulletin board, for a concert that had happened the weekend before.

"Why didn't you come over to say hello to the Wallaces?" David said, as the couple walked away to the parking lot.

"The Wallaces? You mean, from Soren's preschool? Oh, my God." I was mortified. They weren't David's clients; they were parents of Soren's old childhood friend. We hadn't seen them in years. "They must have thought I was so rude!"

Yet while being married to a psychologist can lead to unnerving moments, there is nothing like living in a small town when you're a foster parent.

Alyana had been with us for two months. It was a Sunday afternoon, and we were walking on a paved path by a nearby creek. Lila was on her bike, riding ahead, her fall jacket tied around her waist, flapping out behind her in the wind. David and I were taking turns carrying Alyana. The sun was warm, and I felt content.

For the most part, the transition had been going well. The first few nights Alyana was with us were difficult. She couldn't sleep, and I lay awake next to her for hours while she crawled from the pillow to the foot of the bed, back and forth, over and over. Nothing David or I did helped her settle down. On the third night, she finally fell asleep just after midnight. I dozed off next to her, and at two o'clock in the morning, I woke up to see that she had climbed out of bed and was out in the hallway. Thinking, perhaps, that she was heading toward the bathroom, I followed her. She walked quickly through the dark living room, with me a few steps behind. After moving through the kitchen, she flipped the lock on the handle of the sliding door; she had figured out how to open it for the cat earlier that afternoon. Before I could stop her, she opened the door all the way and took a step outside into the black night. I caught her arm and carried her back to her room. I couldn't imagine where she was going, or what would have happened if I hadn't been there to stop her. After that, we put a baby lock on the inside of the door.

But then, after the first few nights, she began to sleep well. The social worker explained that she had never had a regular routine in her previous life. In her first weeks with us, she seemed to be thriving with a consistent schedule, clear expectations, and lots of affection. That Sunday, on the bike path, Alyana rode on David's shoulders, commenting on the scene as we walked along. We looked and felt like a happy family of four.

"Tee-tee!" she shouted. As an almost three-year-old, Alyana's speech seemed underdeveloped to us. We were still working to decipher some of her words. She would be evaluated by a speech therapist later that month. I assumed she was referring to the birds flying overhead.

"Yes, aren't they pretty," I replied. "Such pretty birds."

We passed a couple who looked at us strangely. Several minutes later, the man in the couple jogged up to us. He had circled back and was panting. "I'm sorry, but would it be possible for Alyana to say hello to her aunt?"

My stomach clenched. Her aunt? Who was Alyana's aunt? The social worker hadn't mentioned anything about extended family being in town.

Alyana was bouncing on David's shoulders. "Tee-Tee! Tee-Tee! Want to see Tee-Tee!" The meaning of her babbling now became clear. Alyana had recognized her aunt.

I wasn't sure how to handle this, what the rules dictated. One of the greatest frustrations about fostering so far had been that the social worker who had been assigned to Alyana's case, Michaela, refused to tell us anything beyond the most basic facts about Alyana's history. She explained that this was the official policy; Social Services only told foster parents the information that might directly impact the day-to-day well-being of the child. Michaela did not believe that the majority of the details about Alyana's background—in particular, information about her parents' lives and their problems—were essential for us to know. I talked with another foster parent who thought this approach was strange; their social worker had told them everything she knew about their foster son, including all the details about his parents that were in the file. I couldn't figure out if the limited disclosure was truly Social Services' strict policy, or just a loose guideline that Michaela had implemented with particular zeal.

The result was that we only knew the basics about Alyana's background, and almost nothing about her extended family. And now, that afternoon by the creek, there was an aunt waiting on the trail up ahead. The man in front of us—the aunt's boyfriend, he explained—looked at us expectantly.

David and I looked at each other. "Well, I think a short visit to say hello would be fine," he said.

I nodded. Alyana didn't seem distressed; we were in a public place. A short visit seemed reasonable.

We stood on the path while Alyana ran to "Tee-Tee," and they embraced. The young woman, Alexis, was in her mid-twenties. She had a Rolling Stone t-shirt on, and a feather tattoo on her arm. Her eyes were filled with tears.

Alyana bounced in her arms. "Tee-Tee! Tee-Tee! I go to a new school."

We introduced each other. Alexis explained that Alyana

had lived with her for about three months when she was a baby.

"But then her mom—she's my half-sister—picked her up one day, unexpectedly. I've only seen them twice since then. I had heard from my cousin that Alyana was in foster care."

We chatted for a few minutes. I tried to keep it light, reporting on our early attempts at potty training and describing the daycare where Alyana had been attending the past six weeks. "She's doing really well," I said, quietly. "We love having her."

"Thank you for letting us say hello." Alexis wiped her cheek. "Okay, Alyana, we need to go to the store. But we love you. I hope we'll get to see you again soon."

"Bye Tee-Tee! Love you!" Alyana was passed back to David's arms and returned to his shoulders. "Bye! Have good day!" she called out to her aunt.

Alexis waved and then turned. Her shoulders were hunched as she walked away, her boyfriend's arm around her.

We resumed our walk. The brief visit had gone well. No drama. Alexis was appropriate, and Alyana didn't seem traumatized. But I was unsettled. I could no longer pretend we were a normal family of four. Alyana had a whole life before she came to us, a history, people who knew and loved her. We loved her, too, but she didn't belong to us.

* * *

At the next court date, the judge determined that Alyana would have weekly supervised visits with her mother, Candace, at Michaela's office. I would help with transportation every Tuesday. David and I first met Candace a week after Alyana had been placed with us. When we told Stacey that we'd accept the foster placement, I had forgotten that ten days later we were scheduled to go on vacation to Vermont. So in addition to scrambling to find daycare for Alyana and making multiple visits to the doctor to address the diaper rash that had been infected when she arrived at our house, our first days of fostering were spent working with Social Services to determine whether Alyana could travel to Vermont with us. The alternative was to put her in respite care—a temporary placement with another foster family while we went on vacation—or to cancel the trip. Both options were unacceptable to me. This was our big annual vacation; my entire family would be there, and there was no way we could skip it. But it was equally unimaginable to consider moving Alyana into another home temporarily while we were gone. Not only could I not bear to contemplate the trauma and disruption that another move—and a temporary one—would cause her, I was already deeply in love with this child. There was no way I was letting her out of my sight. I was in fierce mama bear mode.

So we asked Social Services for permission to take Alyana to Vermont with us. They were okay with the plan. They would give us an official letter, allowing us to cross state lines with a ward of the state. But they wanted us to meet Alyana's mother first. Candace was cooperating with

Social Services; she had a lot of challenges in her personal life, and said she knew she wasn't ready to take care of Alyana yet. She wanted what was best for her daughter, including her safety. Social Services had spoken highly of us, and Candace was apparently glad that Alyana had been placed with us temporarily while she worked to get her life back together. But Candace had never been on an airplane. She was nervous about the idea of Alyana flying, worried about her being so far away. Social Services thought an in-person meeting before we left would help reassure her.

We met her in a small, square room at the county health department. David and I arrived first, and we sat on the couch, holding hands. I tucked my flower-print skirt beneath me, self-consciously. I had just come from work. Was I overdressed for this meeting? Alyana's mother, Candace, arrived a few minutes later, led in by Michaela. She was wearing jeans and a white t-shirt. She was quiet, but didn't seem defensive or angry. We shook hands and made small talk for a few minutes. We gave her a few updates on how Alyana was doing. I told her how much we were enjoying having her with us.

"It's a blessing," I said, and then immediately regretted the words. Probably nothing about this situation felt like a blessing to Alyana's mother.

"I'm glad she's with you." Candace smiled.

We showed her photographs of Lila and Soren, and explained the plan for the vacation in Vermont. Candace nodded. "It sounds like a good opportunity for Alyana.

I want her to have good things. Social Services says she's already really bonded to you. I'm okay if she goes."

We left the meeting with a plan to call Candace every day while we were gone. Candace had just gotten a new cell phone and had started working at a local grocery store. She would get off at 4:00 p.m. each day; calling her any time after that would be fine.

* * *

Each afternoon of the trip, Alyana and I would go into the kitchen of the old cottage where my family vacationed every summer. There was only one phone in the rustic cabin; we didn't get cell phone reception in northern Vermont. I would slide down the door of the old refrigerator until I was sitting on the linoleum floor beside Alyana, and then hand her the phone. She didn't have a long attention span, and the calls were short. Candace seemed fine with the brevity, just glad to touch base with her daughter.

"I love you," Candace said, at the end of each call.

"I love you, too," Alyana replied.

"I love you to the moon and back again," Candace would respond, each day.

Alyana would nod and repeat the words. "To the moon and back."

Once we returned to Chapel Hill, the regular Tuesday afternoon visits with Candace began. Michaela would pick Alyana up at daycare and bring her to her office. Candace and Alyana would spend an hour together, playing in a room that Social Services had set up with toys and an art table. I would pick Alyana up after their visit. For the most part, the visits seemed to go okay. I was irritated when Alyana would emerge from the meeting with a Coke and bag of cookies in hand. It was 5:00 p.m., and the last thing we needed was to have this high-energy child jacked up on caffeine and sugar. But I was mainly worried about how Alyana would handle the transitions. Most weeks, Alyana would go willingly into my arms, but then begin to cry as I walked away. "Goodbye, Mommy! Goodbye!" she would call back to her mother.

"Goodbye, sweetie. Have a good week," Candace would reply, standing on the sidewalk next to Michaela. I would roll down the window as we drove away so Alyana could wave.

"I want my mommy back," she would whimper to me, repeating the statement over and over for the first few minutes of the drive.

But then she would recover, asking for her container of playdough, and playing contentedly the rest of the way back to the house.

"Mommy, is Lila home yet?" Alyana would ask me, looking up as we pulled into the driveway.

I shook my head, amazed at how fluid the concepts of mother and home seemed to be for this little girl.

* * *

As we settled into our new routine, I became increasingly exhausted. Working full-time and parenting two kids is always demanding. On top of that, I felt like I had a part-time job as a case manager; there were appointments with Alyana's psychologist, routine home visits with multiple social workers, phone calls and visits with Candace, meetings with the daycare staff to address concerns about behavior and emotional meltdowns, extra doctor visits to meet the state's requirements for check-ups for foster kids, appointments with specialists to test for possible speech delays and hearing loss.

Overall, Alyana was doing better than I would have expected, but there were challenges. Her teachers called me one day, worried because Alyana had curled into a ball during naptime and started crying out with frantic, animalistic gulps. When they tried to comfort her, her eyes remained unfocused and she seemed far away; they couldn't get her to calm down. On other days, the teachers would report that Alyana seemed to take pleasure in causing other students distress. She would knock down another girl's block castle, and then watch calmly and with interest as the child cried.

At home, Alyana was in constant motion. She had no ability to play on her own, even for a short period. At her age, Soren or Lila could entertain themselves for long stretches of time, engaging with a favorite toy on the carpet, or drawing at the kitchen table while we fixed a meal or washed dishes nearby. Alyana could only concentrate on a game or project if we sat with her and facilitated the entire activity. It was exhausting; we had no downtime.

One Saturday, David organized a babysitter, and for the first time in months, we went out to dinner. I posted a photo on Facebook of us grinning in the car, with the caption, "We escaped!" Laughing about something silly the girls had done that day, we walked to the restaurant, arm-in-arm.

As we turned the corner, there was Candace.

She looked different than during our normal Tuesday afternoon visits. On those days, she was typically dressed in her work uniform or wearing a t-shirt and jeans. That night, she had on a man's leather jacket. She was standing next to a guy, and I assumed it was his. With a cigarette in her hand and silver hoop earrings, she was clearly dressed up for a night out. I was, too, wearing a long vintage red coat over a sparkly dress.

I felt guilty, like I had been caught in the act of abandoning her daughter. "Candace! Hey! How are you?" I said. "We have a babysitter for Alyana. We just wanted to get out of the house for a night."

"Oh, good." She nodded. "You guys definitely deserve a break."

A break? We were paying sixteen dollars an hour for a sitter to watch her daughter and ours so we could get a two-hour reprieve from parenting. The moment felt surreal.

We said our goodbyes and proceeded to the restaurant. I sat, shaken. What was Candace doing tonight? Who was she with? How could she not see the painful irony of the moment?

Most of all, I wondered who I would bump into next in our small college town?

7

Jacqueline

THREE WEEKS LATER, Michaela told us that Social Services was not happy with the progress Candace was making. Given her history, they had also been anticipating this as a possible outcome, and already had a Plan B in mind.

Michaela told us that Alyana had an older brother, Charles. He was twelve and had been legally adopted by Candace's cousin, Jacqueline, three years before. Jacqueline was twenty years older than Candace, and Candace viewed her as a surrogate mother. Jacqueline was like a grandmother to Alyana. Candace and Alyana had lived with Jacqueline briefly at one point when Alyana was about a year old.

Apparently, Jacqueline was frantic to get Alyana out of foster care. She wanted the siblings to be together and to adopt Alyana like she had done with Charles. Michaela and her supervisor were supportive of the plan. They had to complete the background checks and other paperwork, and then Alyana could move. Candace would have a year to try and get her life back together and prove to the court that she was competent enough to regain custody. If not, the backup plan would be that Alyana would stay with Jacqueline and Charles permanently. In the meantime, the sibling pair would be reunited.

I absorbed this news quietly, listening to Michaela's explanation during one of our regular meetings. I was becoming increasingly bonded to Alyana, loving the rhythm of parenting her, despite the stress and exhaustion. One evening that fall, I took Alyana and Lila to the nearby park after dinner. It was dusk and the two girls ran around outside as the light faded. It had rained that afternoon, and the ground was coated with damp, orange leaves. Looking at the two girls, both with long hair streaming behind them as they ran—laughing and calling out to each other as the sky darkened—I felt the rightness of it in that moment. Parenting these two girls felt like a fit for me.

Alyana darted over to me and I picked her up. Coincidentally, we both had on green parkas—hers a hand-me-down from a friend's daughter, mine a gift from my mother. She pushed her forehead against mine. Anyone walking by would have assumed she was my daughter. I rubbed my nose against hers, hugged her to me, and then put her down.

Listening to Michaela's explanation of the transition plan, I knew that Social Services wasn't asking us what we wanted. They weren't offering us the chance to keep Alyana. Their first choice was that any child be with biological family members. We were foster parents. This was temporary. It had always been temporary. This is what we had signed up for.

And more importantly, I had made an explicit agreement with David that we wouldn't adopt.

I realized it was a relief not to be given a choice. David was already suspicious of my intentions, knowing how close I felt to Alyana.

"Just watch," David said. "This placement with Jacqueline will fall through. And when they ask us if we want to adopt, you'll shrug and say, "It's God's will." This whole thing is a set-up for both of us."

I was silent. I didn't want to think about it. The option wasn't on the table. Social Services had not even raised that as a possibility. It wasn't worth considering.

"That's not going to happen," I replied to David. "Jacqueline sounds really steady. She's had Charles for three years. She wants Alyana."

And it did seem like Jacqueline was highly motivated. They lived in Kentucky, seven hours away, but were moving to North Carolina in two months to expedite Alyana's transition. The approval would move more quickly through the court system if Alyana didn't have to cross state lines. Later that month, Jacqueline drove to Chapel Hill to see Alyana and to meet us for the first time.

I brought Alyana to the health department for the visit with Jacqueline. I wasn't sure of the protocol. I assumed Michaela would meet us in the lobby and facilitate introductions. As I turned the corner to the receptionist's desk, Alyana cried out, "Nanna!" Michaela wasn't in sight.

I walked over to the woman that Alyana was waving at. "Jacqueline?" I said.

The woman nodded and opened her arms wide to Alyana. "Darling, hello! How are you?"

I passed Alyana to her.

"Oh, my goodness! You've gotten so big!" She squeezed Alyana, who seemed delighted.

"Hi!" Jacqueline looked at me.

"Hi, I'm Kate. It's great to meet you."

We chatted for ten minutes. I liked Jacqueline immediately. She was funny, open, and down-to-earth.

"My husband, Mike, is in the military," she said. "We live on the base. He's been in the army for twenty-five years. Getting ready to take retirement. He's only forty-nine, so of course he can keep working. He's trained as an electrician and got a good job offer in North Raleigh. I used to be a truck driver, then a bookkeeper." She laughed. "Now I'm a stay-at-home mom. I take care of Charles, of course, and also my husband Mike's two boys from his first marriage. And we have two dogs, Chestnut and Lulu." She had a throaty laugh.

Alyana laid her head on her shoulder.

"I have two grown kids myself. Three grandchildren. I'm like the little old lady who lived in the shoe. Surrounded by kids!" She laughed again.

"I brought you something," she told Alyana. "A quilt I just made for you. Look! It has kitty cats sewn on it, the brown and black kitties you like."

The kitties she liked. I was again reminded that Alyana had a long history; this woman knew what Alyana liked. But I also knew a list of things Alyana liked. Strawberry yogurt in the morning when she first woke up. Parking the car a few blocks away from daycare in the morning so we could walk in together hand-in-hand, looking at the flowers along the sidewalk and talking about the day ahead. Playing the monster chase game with David around the island in the kitchen. Reading the dinosaur book with the flaps with Lila before bed.

Michaela walked up to us. "Oh, good, I'm glad you all connected."

We chatted for a few minutes, and then I left them there. Alyana would visit with Jacqueline for an hour or so, and then Michaela would drive her back to our house.

* * *

Over the next month, my internal monologue went radio silent. Getting through daily tasks, navigating our complicated schedules, it was all I could do. I was accustomed to having a constant mental narrative running at all times, analyzing, reflecting, processing life events. But my mind became like one of those ominous beeping machines at the hospital that has gone silent—all thoughts flatlined. My days at work were incredibly demanding. I was managing two projects which both had big deadlines later that month. Each day, David and I would take turns picking Alyana up at daycare. On my assigned days, I battled through a forty-five minute commute to make it to her in time before they shut down for the night. Often the last parent to arrive, I would find Alyana at the door, waiting worriedly for me. At home, we would cook and clean, play, reprimand, bathe, and then hustle both girls into bed. Then I would get back onto email for another hour or two to finish up work tasks, trying to reserve twenty minutes before bed to catch up with David before we both collapsed. I couldn't think about anything, especially the transition that was looming.

At church one Sunday, I slumped in my pew, exhausted. Both the girls had been deposited in Sunday school. With Alyana's arrival, it took a herculean effort to get us all dressed and to church on time. It was nothing like it used to be when it was just Lila and me. Back then, I'd tell Lila to slip on a sundress, and we'd be out the door in ten minutes.

Yet despite the effort and frazzled nerves, I loved bringing Alyana to church. She had lots of fans. When we arrived each Sunday, she would look for Stephen, a grandfatherly gentleman who was particularly kind to her. When she spotted him, she would wave eagerly and shout out to everyone, "That's my friend!" Church ladies cooed at her. Alyana was adorable, and I received admiring, appreciative looks from parishioners as they passed us in the hallway.

The previous week I had asked some women at church to pray for us, telling them that we were expecting Alyana to transition to her new home in a few months.

"Oh, dear! Why can't you just adopt her?" one of the women said, in a kind voice.

I grimaced and looked down. "We're just fostering."

That morning in the pew, I was grateful for the twenty minutes of quiet before I would need to retrieve the girls. But just as I was picking up my hymnal, a mother and her son sat in front of me. He was already fidgeting in his seat. Similar to my proclivity for choosing the slowest moving line at the checkout in any store, I seem to have a knack for sitting behind the loudest, most unruly children at church. I closed my eyes, trying to grow still and allow some peace to seep into me. I tried to remember Carl McColman's words that we have to come to church because being in "community [is] the essential starting point" for a spiritual life. But the boy's restlessness intensified. He started kicking the seat and then began murmuring a string of complaints. Why wasn't the mother taking him outside, I wondered, increasingly irritated. Her angry whispers weren't working. My blood pressure was rising; surely hers was, too. Couldn't she give us both some relief and walk her son to the back where there were rocking chairs set up for families with fussy kids?

Finally, the boy, who was arguing about a half-finished Lego project in his hand, held up the toy in the air and half-whispered, half-yelped, "I need help!"

Those three words seemed to stop everything. The boy

and his mother ceased struggling. He leaned against her shoulder, and her arm went around him. He was still for most of the rest of the service. My muscles released, and the sermon I had been straining to hear was eclipsed by those three words hanging in the air: "I need help." I realized that the boy had offered the real teaching I needed that day.

"I need help," I whispered, not sure if I was talking to myself or to God. "I don't want to let her go."

8
Thanksgiving

CHARLES LOOKED JUST LIKE ALYANA. He had the same dark eyes, the same blond hair that curled in wavy slants across his forehead. And it was obvious that Alyana adored her brother. The devotion radiated in her eyes the moment we walked through the door. We were visiting Jaqueline at their new house in North Raleigh, forty-five minutes from our house. They had moved a week before, and there were boxes stacked in the hallway and against the living room walls. Over the past two months, we had scheduled weekly Skype video calls with Jaqueline and Charles. Alyana would hold her toy snake up to the camera on my phone, pretending it was lunging out to bite her brother through the screen. Each time, he would collapse onto the floor, Jacqueline following his descent with her camera,

Alyana squealing with delight. They would do it over and over again. She could never get enough, and Charles never seemed to lose his patience for the game.

Now we settled in for an afternoon visit in the three-bedroom house they were renting on a cul-de-sac. While I bent to pat Lulu, the dog in the fenced-in backyard, and David chatted with Jacqueline, Alyana scampered off with Charles. A few minutes later, a Nerf missile whistled through the door and hit Lila on the back. Lila rushed to join them, and soon we were all involved in an epic battle, with David, Alyana, and Lila on one team, Charles and me on another, and Jaqueline laughing as she drank iced tea and smoked a cigarette from her seat on the sidelines.

I collapsed next to her on a plastic lawn chair. "Whew, they're giving me a workout."

"I know. You wind Charles up in the morning and he doesn't stop all day. He's like the Energizer Bunny. Keeps going and going." She shook her head.

I thought about Alyana's own level of activity and wondered about the biological component of her relentless energy. Jacqueline laughed again as she watched David dive behind the grill to avoid a shot from Charles, and then fired back over the metal cover.

"I honestly didn't think you all would approve of guns," she said.

The comment gave me pause. Jacqueline had mentioned several times that they were "military people." Was there some easy give-away that we were classic, pro-gun-control liberals? Could she also tell at a glance that we bought organic vegetables, wanted universal healthcare coverage, supported immigration reform? Were we that transparent?

"Oh, actually Lila has the same Nerf gun at home," I replied. "She did a surprise attack on us the other day. Kept shooting at us from up in her tree house."

Jacqueline laughed.

In that moment, I was aware of the improbability of the relationship. If it hadn't been for Alyana, I would likely never be having iced tea with someone like Jacqueline— former truck driver, pro-gun military wife—while she lit her third cigarette. I wouldn't see and feel all the things we had in common—the Nerf guns, irreverent senses of humor, the love we had for these kids. I wouldn't have gotten to experience all the ways we enjoyed each other's company, chatting about plans for our backyard gardens, discussing our favorite TV shows, talking about her mother and mine. I was reminded that the word "neighbor" comes from the word near. Jesus calls us to love our neighbors as ourselves, but it can be hard to love someone if you're not near them—physically or emotionally. In that moment, I was struck again by the ways that fostering had changed our lives, connecting and drawing us near to people we never would have otherwise known.

* * *

Several weeks after our visit with Jacqueline, Candace invited us to Thanksgiving dinner. She handed us the flyer as we were leaving Michaela's office on a Tuesday afternoon. The weekly supervised visits had started up again after the social worker had arranged transportation for her. The yellow flyer was an invitation for a free Thanksgiving dinner at the large Methodist church downtown. The meal was intended for the homeless community. Candace didn't have stable housing. She was inviting us to come to the dinner as her guests.

We arrived that Saturday evening and found Candace in the crowd in the basement of the church. She was one of the few women in the group and younger than most of the people there. We lined up with the rest and filled our plates with turkey slices, green bean casserole, and salad made with iceberg lettuce. Candace asked for an extra serving of mashed potatoes from the college student who was dishing them out. Lila got herself a glass of fruit punch, and we all sat together at a long, rectangular folding table. Looking around the room, I wondered what the hosts made of us. I was in brown corduroy pants and a faded blue fleece jacket that my mother-in-law had given me for my birthday seven years before. David was wearing a plaid flannel work shirt. The only obvious clue that we didn't belong was the hand-painted earrings my mother had bought me at a cute boutique that summer, in Vermont. I surreptitiously slipped them out of my ears and stuck them in my pocket. Still, it seemed like we looked a lot more like the people serving the food than the ones in the receiving line.

Alyana sat in Candace's lap, eating from her plate, bouncing up and down. David started a game of tabletop ice cube football with the girls, letting them slide squares of ice across the surface, aiming for the goal formed between his fingers. A man named Sean stopped by and gave Alyana a hug. He took a photo of Candace and Alyana with a disposable camera.

"Sean has been like a brother to me most of my life," Candace said, as Sean walked away. "I owe him twenty bucks, though, so he's kind of annoyed at me right now." She laughed, not seeming concerned.

I wondered about the relationship. How did Candace know this man? What was the nature of their history and bond? Why were they both homeless now? What did the future hold for each of them?

The organizers of the dinner invited everyone to join for optional prayer and Bible study after we were done eating. We waited to see what Candace would do, wanting to follow her lead.

She shook her head. "I'm Southern Baptist," she said, as if that explained why she didn't want to join.

Instead, we sat on the benches in the hallway outside. Alyana ran up and down, dodging our legs, which we held up in an improvised obstacle course. She giggled each time she ducked away and avoided being grabbed by one of us in a scissor hold.

I felt grateful that Candace had invited us that evening. Yet again we were guests in a place and space we never would have been if it hadn't been for fostering. I was reminded of what Marcus Borg calls the "table fellowship" of Jesus. Borg explains that in Jesus' time, sharing a meal held tremendous social meaning. He writes that the "Pharisees (and others) would not eat with somebody who was impure, and no decent person would share a meal with an outcast." In contrast, "The meals of Jesus embodied his alternative vision for an inclusive community…negating the boundaries of the purity system." Jesus' community included "women, untouchables, the poor, the maimed, and the marginalized," and as such, "the inclusiveness of Jesus' movement embodied a radically alternative social vision."

I watched as Alyana and Lila sat on the floor, whispering to one another. "Thank you for inviting us tonight," I said to Candace.

"Yeah, I'm really glad that you came," she replied. "And I'm, uh, I want to say that I'm really thankful for what a great job you're doing taking care of Alyana."

I was surprised. "Oh, we've been really glad to have the time with Alyana. We really love her."

The moment didn't feel awkward. It felt like we were expressing genuine gratitude for one another.

"Yeah, it definitely takes a village to raise a kid," Candace replied.

Just then, Sean showed back up. He had gone down the street to CVS and had used their one-hour service to develop the photos from his disposable camera. He gave us a copy of the one with Candace and Alyana sitting together at dinner. In the picture, Alyana was wearing Candace's baseball cap balanced on her head. Alyana had put it there just before the photograph was taken, insisting, "I wear the hat!"

As we were leaving, after Alyana had hugged Candace goodbye, I gave Alyana the photo to hold. She stared at it raptly as we walked out, waving back distractedly at her mother over my shoulder, only after I prompted her.

* * *

In the parking lot, David was livid.

"It takes a village? A village!" He fumed as we got into the car. "She's abdicated all responsibility for her daughter, and all she can do is shrug and say, 'It takes a village?' That is the most ridiculous thing I have ever heard."

I was surprised at my even-tempered husband's anger. Certainly, he'd heard many worse things in his professional life. Candace's comment felt benign to me. And I personally didn't feel any anger toward her. She clearly had a challenging life, but she wasn't malicious and seemed to want what was best for Alyana. I got the sense that she just couldn't do much more. What was the point of being angry? But maybe that was the wrong attitude. Maybe I ought to have higher expectations.

As I was putting Alyana to bed that night, I taped the photo of her and Candace on the wall near her pillow. She touched the image of her mother. In the picture, they had the same smile, the same round cheekbones. I was reminded of Charles. During our visit to Raleigh, Jacqueline had told us that Charles had attended dozens of different elementary schools between kindergarten and fourth grade.

"He bounced from location to location for years. Never had any sense of stability. She put him in some terrible situations." I could hear the disgust in Jacqueline's voice as she watched Charles playing in the backyard.

It was the first negative thing Jacqueline had said about Candace since we had met them. She had always been discreet. Charles' history had come up because I had asked whether he liked his new school.

"It's so good for him to be on the football team," she said. "A perfect outlet for his energy. He loves it."

Her gaze still on Charles, Jacqueline took another drag from her cigarette and sighed.

9

The Skin
of His Face Shone

THE IMAGE IN THE TITLE FOR THIS BOOK came to me three
years before I knew we would become foster parents,
long before I had any idea that I might write about our
journey. I was in the middle of writing my first book—a
memoir about my conversion to Christianity and the first
year following my baptism. There were no plans for a
second book; I could still barely believe I was writing the
first one. Yet one Sunday morning, I was sitting at church
listening to the sermon, and there it was.

The preacher was a young woman—a friend of mine
who had recently graduated from divinity school and had

been ordained as an Episcopal priest two months before. She was slim and pretty, with a sweet smile and a quiet, peaceful presence that always calmed me when we were together. She was preaching on the passage about Moses. How he came down from the mountain and how the skin of his face shone because he had been talking with God. In that moment, with a strange and inexplicable jolt of clarity, I knew the image would help form the title for my second book. It made no sense. There was no plan, no vision for such a project. I had no inkling of what the narrative would be or why I might write it. But still, there it was. The title. Hanging in the air above me, almost if I could reach out and touch it.

The words lodged in my heart as my friend continued her sermon. What was this, I wondered? What did it mean to have skin that became shiny because of God?

* * *

I looked down at my phone. Michaela's number showed up on the screen; I had just missed her call. We had seen her the day before at the psychologist's office. Alyana had been with us for five months, and we had a group meeting to start planning her transition. Most of the boxes were unpacked at Jaqueline's house. Christmas was coming up. They were ready for her. The psychologist insisted that the transition had to be gradual. Alyana was bonded to us; this was obvious to her from our sessions together. Things were going well at daycare. She wanted the move to be a smooth as possible. I nodded as I listened to her. My stomach was tight. *As smooth as possible.*

Michaela's missed call probably meant that she wanted to discuss additional details about the plan. I called her back after stepping out of my meeting at work.

"Hi, what's up?" I said.

"There's a problem. Jacqueline is in the hospital. She tripped when she was taking care of her grandson this morning. Fell down half a flight of stairs. She shattered her knee. She'll have surgery tomorrow. The doctor says she'll be okay, but the recovery is going to take a while. Alyana will need to stay with you for at least four more months."

Four months. I exhaled sharply. A reprieve.

I drove home. We will have her for Christmas, we will have her for Christmas.

The words kept running through my mind as I made my way back to the house. With Jacqueline's permission, we had already gotten Alyana a new bicycle as a gift. The plan had been to let her open it at Jacqueline's house; we were going to bring it over that weekend so it would be under their tree. When I got home, I went out to the shed to look at the bike again. Yes, there would be space between the couch and our Christmas tree for it. It would fit. I smiled.

* * *

Christmas morning was a hectic gluttony of gifts. I had spent the week before in a rush of supplemental shopping. I knew I had gone overboard, and as was to be expected, both Lila and Alyana ended up in tears by the afternoon. But still, it was our day—a Christmas together. We were an unusual, impermanent family, but one full of love.

I was off work that week, and I felt pressure to make the time special. After further consultation with the doctors, it turned out that Jacqueline wouldn't need surgery. Just some pins in her knee and time to heal. In the meantime, we called her on Skype each morning, and then filled the days with holiday activities, the girls eagerly scooping out globs of homemade icing onto sugar cookies and eating popcorn in front of the fire while we read stories together. Midway through the break, it snowed and we spent the afternoon outside. Lila and Alyana sat together on the plastic sled we borrowed from a neighbor. Sitting together in their puffy winter jackets, a small green blob in front of a pink one, they tore down the hill, laughing, and returned to the top again and again.

That night, David and I lay in bed together, reading. Both girls were asleep. David pushed up on his elbows and looked down at me. He made a joke and his eyes crinkled as he grinned; they shut almost entirely whenever he smiled. It was the face I loved, the cheeks and chin and lips. It was the face I had looked at every day for more than fifteen years.

I inhaled sharply. I looked at him more closely and realized: it was David. His skin shone. David's face shone with love and with generosity. With faith and with sacrifice. With all of the things he had demonstrated by becoming a foster parent with me.

I had been so angry at him for so long because I had wanted another baby after Lila was born and he didn't. We had debated the issue for years. Fostering had been our compromise, despite his misgivings. He had said yes, which allowed us to embark on this crazy, unexpected, bittersweet, love-filled journey. He was the protagonist I had been looking for to match the story I was writing.

"Thank you," I whispered.

He pulled me to him. The house was quiet.

10

Easter

THE REST OF THE WINTER AND SPRING went by quickly. Life was full, and we were busy. The rhythm of our days regained a sense of normalcy. The biggest surprise came a few weeks after Christmas when Michaela called.

"I have some news." I held the phone steady against my ear, wondering if Jacqueline's leg was worse or if Candace had to cancel our Tuesday visit that week.

"Candace is pregnant."

"What?"

My mind slowed. As Michaela talked, I had difficulty listening, trying to process the details. Candace was four months pregnant. She had known for a while, but now she was starting to show. Alyana might notice or have questions that week during their visit. Michaela wanted us to be prepared.

My mind flashed to a moment a few weeks before Christmas. I had been shopping with Alyana for new shoes in the small mall near our house. I turned the corner and there was Candace and her new boyfriend.

"Hi. Ah, how...how are you?" I stumbled over the words. Alyana was on my hip. Even at three years old, her petite body was still light enough to carry easily.

Alyana reached eagerly for her mother, and I handed her over.

"We were just looking at shoes," I said. "Do you...do you want to join us?"

We spent the next twenty minutes trying on sneakers together. First, the white ones with glittery, light-up bottoms. I cringed; the soles were impractically thick, but Alyana squealed with delight when she saw them, and Candace nodded appreciatively as they lit up with each step. Next we tried on the black ones with rainbow laces. During the entire visit, Candace boyfriend's stood silently by. I had introduced myself as we entered the store, but he hadn't offered his name, just a handshake and a nod. Candace was warm and chatty, but her companion was oddly silent. I wondered about him as we stood together in the aisle of the shoe store. What was his story?

After some discussion, Alyana agreed that the black shoes were more comfortable, and we headed to the counter to pay.

"Alyana, I need to say goodbye now," Candace said, after the cashier handed me the receipt. She hugged Alyana and handed her back to me. "I have to go to the grocery store, but I'll see you soon. I love you. To the moon and back."

Alyana cried quietly against my shoulder as I carried her away. I kept my voice upbeat, trying to distract her with promises that we'd stop at the library on the way home. She could pick out three new books; maybe we'd get another Maisey Mouse story. The one with the alphabet rhyme we had seen the week before. Alyana kept crying, her fingers digging into my shoulder.

Michaela's voice brought me back to the moment. "Don't tell Alyana about the pregnancy. Candace will tell her. I just wanted you to be prepared."

That Tuesday after her afternoon visit with Candace, Alyana came home bouncy. "There's a baby in my mommy's tummy! I'm going to be a big sister!" she told me.

"Yes, that's so exciting," I nodded and hugged her.

She quickly became distracted by a toy and didn't mention it again the rest of the evening.

"What is the plan? What's going to happen to Candace and the baby?" David asked Michaela during our scheduled home visit three days later.

Michaela sighed and ran her hand through her hair. "We stick with the current plan. Candace has a long way to go. She needs stable housing, a job. She has to demonstrate to us that she can successfully take care of this baby before we would even consider giving her custody of Alyana. So Alyana will still transition to Jacqueline's house."

I nodded. "Yes, Jacqueline seems great. I think that will be a stable and loving home for Alyana."

"Yes, and her leg is improving, " Michaela said. "We can start working on the transition plan."

* * *

So that spring, we started to implement a gradual transition, guided by the therapist, Deborah, whom Alyana had been seeing weekly. Alyana started with day-long visits at Jacqueline's house, and then an overnight stay. Alyana was delighted to be there, thrilled for the chance to play with Charles, and full of affection for Jacqueline. But we hadn't told her yet that she would be moving; I didn't know how she would respond or if she would even understand.

That was the week that Alyana spontaneously yelled out, "I love this family!" one evening as I strapped her into her booster for dinner. Lila grinned and gave her a kiss on the cheek.

"Mommy, can I have red sauce on my noodles?" Alyana asked me.

That week, David and I met with the therapist alone, and I asked the question that had been haunting me since Alyana first arrived. "I just don't understand this model," I said. "It doesn't make sense to me. Alyana's completely bonded to us, and we're totally bonded with her. How is this good for her? To love so deeply and then to lose it all again? It seems more damaging to her—another trauma, another loss. I'm not saying we should keep her, but I don't understand. Has being with us ultimately been good for her?"

"Would you have wanted her to be with a foster family that was distant and indifferent?" The therapist looked at me carefully. "Once a person learns the skills of loving and experiences that type of connection, she can transfer that ability to other people, other relationships. It's much more damaging to never experience a loving attachment at all."

I nodded. I guessed that made sense. Sort of. I could concede that it was better to love and lose than to never love at all. But so much loss, so much change for a three-year-old—it seemed unbearable. I couldn't help worrying that by adoring her, by pulling her so deep into our hearts and our lives, that we had made things worse.

* * *

Three weeks before Alyana was scheduled to move, Jacqueline and I had a phone date. I needed to go over some logistics with her. I was proud that my voice didn't quaver as I asked about a plan for moving Alyana's clothes and toys over to their house. I was keeping it together. Sticking to the plan.

"So how are you feeling?" I asked her.

"Honestly, I feel terrible." Jacqueline's voice grew thick on the phone. "I feel so guilty about taking Alyana from you."

My breath caught. I was silent.

"I've never told you. But I lost a child when I was young. When I was fifteen, I—something bad happened to me. I was raped."

I inhaled.

"I got pregnant. I was too young, and so I gave the baby away. He was adopted by a nice couple. A pastor and his wife. I never saw him. Never saw him his whole life. But I loved him so much." Jacqueline began crying.

"Oh, my God, I'm so sorry."

Jacqueline took a deep breath. "The family contacted me when he turned fourteen. We talked on the phone twice. He asked questions, asked why I had given him away. I told him I loved him so much, told him that I did it so that he could have a better life. He said he understood. He said that he wanted to meet me. So we planned to see each other. We were all going to get together for dinner at a restaurant near the beach where they lived." Jacqueline paused. "Later that month, there was an accident. The family was in a car wreck. The car flipped over twice. My son died. He died on the side of the road. I never got to meet him."

"Oh, my God, Jacqueline. I am so, so sorry." I couldn't believe what I was hearing.

Jacqueline continued, "So I know what it's like to lose a child. And I hate that I'm taking Alyana from you. I feel so guilty. I know you're her mother." I could hear a sob rise and then be stifled, choked back into her throat.

In that moment, I could feel the hugeness of the choice I had to make. I could feel the temptation. I could use the moment to hold on more tightly to my own grief. In an unobtrusive way, I could leverage Jacqueline's guilt to justify and cement my own experience of impending loss. I would do it gracefully, of course, acknowledging the enormity of her pain first. And then I could allow my own grief to be categorized—by her remorse and with my consent—in the way she was offering. Or I could let her off the hook.

I took a deep breath. "Actually, Jacqueline, you are helping me. David and I agreed at the beginning of all of this that we wouldn't adopt. Our commitment is to foster. I made an explicit agreement with him that this would be temporary. If you gave me the opportunity to keep Alyana, it would create a huge crisis in our marriage. I love David, and I don't know what we would do. I don't know how we would handle it. It would be terrible. So this is helping us. It's good. Alyana loves you and Charles so much. She should be with her brother. It's okay."

Jacqueline's breath came out fast as a half-laugh, half-whimper. She paused, and I heard her cigarette lighter click.

"Okay, well, we really want you and David to stay in her life. When we get legal guardianship, I want to make you the godparents. Officially. I want you to take her if anything happens to me and Mike. I want her to know she always has you. Will you consider it?"

"Of course! We would be honored." I exhaled.

I had done it. I could feel that my response was a release for both Jacqueline and me. I felt as though I had survived a challenge, a test of character. And Jacqueline was offering us a way forward. A gift. We had already talked about wanting to stay in each other's lives, that we would visit regularly. But to be legal godparents—this was more than

I had hoped for.

"I'm grateful to know you," I told Jacqueline. "I'm really lucky."

"Me, too." She inhaled.

"I'm so sorry for what happened to your son. To you," I said, quietly.

"Yeah. I guess this is why I'm like the old lady who lives in a shoe. Why I keep taking on these kids. My heart just breaks for them."

"Mine does, too."

During the conversation, I had moved out to our balcony. It was getting late. I looked up at the stars. I knew Jacqueline was out on her back porch, smoking her cigarette. The thirty-seven miles between us seemed to be both an enormous distance and nothing at all. I could almost see the smoke from her cigarette curling up in the night sky.

* * *

Jacqueline, her husband, Mike, and Charles came to our house for Easter. Mike's two children from his previous marriage were with their mother. After the meal and a backyard Easter egg hunt, Jacqueline and Mike would pack up the rest of Alyana's stuff—and take her to their home. Her home.

Jacqueline, Mike, and Charles fixed themselves plates of food in our kitchen. I had tried to keep the Easter meal simple. Soup and salad for the adults, bread and cookies from the store. I put a pan of fried hot dogs for the kids on the stovetop. We all sat down to eat.

We had told Alyana a week before that she would be moving in with Jacqueline's family. She seemed unperturbed, but we weren't sure if she fully understood. We bought her a special suitcase with a handle that she could pull herself. We let her pick it out, and she chose the one with pink and yellow flowers. We had taken a load of stuff over the weekend before, including the bike we had gotten her for Christmas. Now there was a pile of toys, a bag of books, and the suitcase waiting by the door in our hallway.

The symbolism of the timing was hard to ignore—Easter. It was the day that made the most sense for the transition, given other scheduling considerations, but I couldn't help but roll my eyes at God every time I thought about it. Could God get any more obvious? Death and resurrection? Loss and rebirth? "Okay, God, I hear you. Or at least I'm trying," I murmured angrily, as I sliced carrots for the salad.

Alyana was also leaving almost nine months from the day she had arrived. Time for a full pregnancy. I thought about all the ways Alyana had grown and changed during the time she had been with us. She had been potty trained. She had read her first word—*stop*—on the sign by our house. Her words changed from being semi-comprehensible most of the time to being fully understandable all of the time. She had been on her first trip to the zoo, her first airplane flight, had her first dentist appointment. We had a basket full of her drawings and other art projects in our closet. Her "good listening" sticker chart was hanging in the kitchen, halfway filled. Over the months, David had added lines on the door in our den, marking her height every few months. Now, next to Lila's snake of upward climbing dashes was Alyana's smaller line, with dates beside the marks. It was strange to think that Alyana's line would remain in our den but would not grow any higher.

As the Easter lunch progressed, I only had to excuse myself once to go to the bathroom, sucking back tears and breathing deeply to center myself. But otherwise, I stayed upbeat, cheerfully hustling the group through the meal and the Easter egg hunt.

While David watched the kids count their candy in the living room, I made up my mind. I approached Jacqueline and whispered, "Can I share a cigarette with you in the backyard?"

"What? You smoke?" she said, incredulous.

"Just once in a while. Don't tell Lila."

My best friend in high school had taught me how to smoke, and I still indulged a few times a year.

The two of us hid behind the gazebo in the backyard.

"I feel like a teenager." Jacqueline giggled. "I haven't snuck a cigarette in thirty years."

I laughed.

And then it was time. Time to say goodbye.

I pulled Charles into a hug. "Thanks for being such a great brother."

"Thanks for being a great mom." He looked into my

eyes.

I hugged him again, blinking away tears. I couldn't believe his poise. He was taking all of this in stride, handling the situation with the emotional grace of an adult. Jacqueline's husband, Mike, in contrast, seemed awkward in our house. He had stayed quiet during most of the lunch, though he was sweet with Alyana. She had climbed in his lap twice and called him Papa. He stroked her hair affectionately, and talked briefly about his job when we asked how it was going. He had been gone during most of our visits, working long shifts, Jacqueline explained.

Mike carried out the last of Alyana's bags and boxes from our front hallway to their car.

"Okay, sweet girl, it's time to go to Nana's house," I said to Alyana.

"Okay, bye-bye." Alyana seemed excited, eager to leave.

I couldn't tell if she thought she was going temporarily for a fun sleepover, or if she really understood what was happening.

"Alyana, sweetie, remember you're going to live at Nana's house now."

"Okay, Mommy. Bye-bye. I love you."

I passed Alyana to David, who hugged her and then handed her into Lila's arms. Alyana squirmed away and ran after Charles, into the car. Jacqueline reached down to strap her into her car seat.

David shouted out after them. "Alyana! What's your middle name?"

It was a running joke between them. Months before,

David had told Alyana that her middle name was Peanut. She loved it, and he repeated the joke often. It exasperated me because she seemed to think he was serious, and I was worried about the confusion we could cause. "No," I would reply each time. "Your middle name is Marcy. Not Peanut. That's just a joke," I would tell her, firmly.

Alyana would laugh and shake her head. "No, my middle name is Peanut!"

Now, as we stood by the front door, David calling out the question to her, Alyana pulled away from Jacqueline and climbed across Charles' lap. She stuck her head out of the car door and pumped her fist into the air.

"Peanut!" she cried back.

And then her head disappeared back again.

We laughed.

David shook his head. "That girl has a hell of a sense of timing."

We waved as they pulled out of the driveway and slowly drove away.

PART THREE

Disruption

11

News

THE FIRST INDICATION that things weren't going well at Jacqueline's house came in October.

Up until then, things had been challenging but bearable for all of us. Alyana seemed to be handling the transition fairly well. Jacqueline reported that there were behavior problems and tearful meltdowns on a regular basis. But Alyana's mood was often sunny, and she seemed to like her new daycare and delighted in her relationship with Charles.

I was holding up better than I had expected. I felt a strange combination of grief and acceptance. I was surprised at my own equanimity. I told a girlfriend that I think people generally assume fostering will have one of two emotional outcomes for the foster parents when the child leaves: either the foster parents will feel relief when a profoundly troubled child who tests all limits moves on, or foster parents will be devastated when a child of their heart is taken from them. Fear of the latter reaction is why I think more people don't or won't consider fostering. An acquaintance once told me that she admired what we were doing, but she would be terrified of the heartbreak that seemed inevitable. Before Alyana came, I shared this concern. I was afraid that the disruption fostering could cause would seriously damage us. That having a child in the house whose behavior was so terrible, or letting go of a child we adored, would be so destabilizing that it would threaten our own family's peace.

And so while I felt a deep grief about Alyana's departure and I missed her every day, I was also relieved that we seemed to be intact emotionally, both as a family and individually.

But then Jacqueline called me one evening. A month after Alyana left us, Candace had given birth to a baby girl, Kaila. But Candace still didn't have a stable housing situation, so upon discharge from the hospital, Kaila would be placed in foster care as well. Jacqueline said that she would take the baby, rather than having her placed with strangers.

David and I worried about the decision—worried that with the addition of the baby, Jacqueline would be overextended. She had Candace's three kids, plus two from Mike's first marriage, and her health was compromised. She was still limping from her knee injury. She smoked two packs of cigarettes a day, and she had revealed to us that she was a survivor of breast and ovarian cancer. But when we went to visit—to take Alyana to the park for a playdate, or to have hotdogs with them in the backyard to celebrate Charles' birthday—she seemed to be holding it together. Kaila was an easy baby, and she sat amiably in her bouncy seat while Jacqueline orchestrated the family's activities.

So Jacqueline's phone call caught me off guard. "I don't think I can do it anymore," she said. "Things are falling apart."

"What?" I asked, alarmed.

"Mike and I are breaking up. Things haven't been right for years."

I pulled the car over into the parking lot of an Applebee's. I had been driving when Jacqueline called and had put her on speaker phone, assuming she just wanted to chat to catch up.

"I just can't do it anymore. We're getting a divorce. I'm not going to have any money. I'm going to need to get a job."

My mind was racing. Jacqueline had never mentioned any of this before. I could hear her take a deep inhale of her cigarette.

"I don't think I can keep the kids."

I told her I was on my way home and would call her back later that night.

"No problem, honey. I just wanted you to know."

She just wanted me to know? What was the plan now?

What would happen to Alyana and Kaila?

I called David and briefly relayed the news. "We'll talk more when I get home."

"Okay," he said, and we hung up.

As I drove home, my heart did a secret leap. I was afraid to think the thoughts that lurked at the outer edges of my brain. But then, as I drove home, I allowed myself to indulge in the question that I had kept at bay all the months that Alyana had been with us: If we had the opportunity, would I want to adopt her? The answer was immediately there in me, with certainty: Of course I wanted Alyana back. If Jacqueline couldn't keep her, I wanted her.

Was there any reason to hope? Could Alyana be ours again?

Then my stomach muscles tightened. Even if it was a possibility, I knew David would never agree. If I wanted to advocate for this, I would have to be braced for a fight.

When I walked through the front door, David was sitting in the den. He wasn't doing anything. He wasn't holding his phone or a magazine. His hands were in his lap.

"How are you?" I said.

"Fine. Tired. Worried about Alyana," he said, quietly.

"I know. Me, too."

His face looked sad, his eyes dark and somber. "I'm not going to let her go back out there. I can't have her sent to some distant, marginal relative. I can't do that."

"But I thought you didn't want to adopt," I was startled. This was not how I imagined the conversation would begin.

"I don't. I do not want to adopt. I have been parenting for over twenty years. I don't feel like I have it in me. But I can't let her go into some horrible situation. This is Alyana we're talking about. I love her."

"Well, we can talk with Michaela as a first step—see what she says." I paused. "How do you feel?"

"I feel angry." His voice was quiet. "I'm not angry at Jacqueline or you. I am just really angry. This is not the life I want."

I looked at David, alarmed. I heard something in his tone that I didn't recognize. A resignation, a stoniness. I felt fear, fear of what this could mean for him, that he would be trapped in a life-long commitment he didn't want. This was the man I loved. I wanted him to be happy.

"Wait a minute, wait a minute," I said. "I think we're getting ahead of ourselves. This is the first time we've ever gotten this message from Jacqueline. Maybe she's just having a hard day. And even if she does divorce Mike, they've been married for over ten years. She'll be eligible for alimony and child support. She needs to advocate for herself."

In that moment, I realized that helping keep the placement with Jacqueline intact was the priority. The current situation was good for everyone. Alyana was with her family, and we got to see her regularly. David wouldn't be backed into a corner. Rather than trying to capitalize on this moment to negotiate for Alyana's return, maybe I could help Jacqueline work out a plan and stabilize things.

"That's true," David said. "She's told us that Mike makes really good money. She definitely needs to advocate for alimony." His face relaxed.

We kept talking. I texted a friend who is an attorney, and she and I talked after dinner. She laid out some options that Jacqueline could consider. When I called Jacqueline back that night, I gave her the list. The volume of her voice increased when she heard the suggestions.

"I guess the bigger question is, though, would you want to keep the kids if you could manage it financially?" I asked her.

"Yes, I really do want them. I love them. Alyana's my girl, my little buddy. I love lying with her in bed, watching a movie after the baby's asleep. I love getting up with her in the morning, walking downstairs together, getting her morning cup of juice. I'm teaching her to tie her shoes. She's a whole lot of trouble, but I love her. It breaks my heart to pieces to think about losing them. I'm sick over it. I can't sleep."

"Well, I really think you should explore your legal options. Will you call a lawyer to talk it through?"

"I will. Thank you. I feel a whole lot better."

"Good, I'm glad. I'm sorry about you and Mike, but I think you have options."

Jacqueline texted me two days later. She had spoken to the lawyer, who agreed that her case looked optimistic.

"I changed my mind," Jacqueline's message concluded. "I want to keep the kids. I'm going to fight for them and for us."

* * *

After that, things were quiet. Jacqueline reported that life was better in their house. Mike had taken a temporary assignment in Dallas, and was sending checks home to Jacqueline each month. They filed for a separation, and she had hired the attorney. She had her hands full, she said, but her knee felt better and the kids were doing well with school. We visited each month, and for the most part the time together went well.

One Saturday, we took Alyana out to pizza and she asked, "When are we going back to our family's house?"

"You mean, back to Nana's house?" I said.

"No, back to *our* family's house," she replied.

It was painful for me. But I was glad things were better for Jacqueline, and I was relieved that David and I hadn't been forced to make what would have been an impossible decision.

Then one evening in February, Michaela called.

"Jacqueline changed her mind again," she said.

David and I had her on speaker phone. We looked at one another.

"She says she can't keep Alyana or Kaila. She'll keep Charles because she's already his legal custodian. She says it's just too much to keep all three of them. She and I met for over an hour today. I'm disappointed. We invested a lot in this transition. But she said that this is her final decision. So we need to make another plan. When this happens, we call it a "disruption." We've officially changed the status in the younger kids' charts."

David and I were both quiet. I couldn't believe this was

happening. I had been naïve; I really thought things were on track with Jacqueline.

Michaela continued, "As you know, we usually like to keep siblings together. But since you have such a strong bond with Alyana, we're going to make an exception in this case and offer you the opportunity to have her come back to you. We know you don't feel like you have the capacity to take two kids, so we would put Kaila with another family. And we're anticipating this would be a permanent placement for both kids. If you take Alyana back, it would almost certainly be to adopt her. Can you let us know your decision early next week?"

It was Friday evening. Michaela had just left the office and was calling us on her way home.

"Of course," David replied.

"If you don't feel like you can take her, we'll need to move forward with selecting another placement. My supervisor and I started looking at the list today, and there are some great couples who are ready to adopt. And we would be sure to choose a family that lives near you so that you can stay in Alyana's life. So don't feel any pressure to take her back if you feel it's not right for your family."

No pressure. I looked at David. What were we going to do?

12
Volcano

I LEARNED EARLY IN MY RELATIONSHIP with David that I was not allowed to yell. Growing up, my brothers and I fought constantly. We would slam doors, shout at each other, storm off in tearful rages. My brothers and I were never allowed to say *I hate you* to one another, and we couldn't curse. But other forms of shouting were permissible, if not desirable. The kids yelled at each other, and my parents yelled at us to quit it.

With David, it was different. Once, after we had been living together a few months, a disagreement escalated and I shouted angry words, slamming the door as I fled outside into the garden. An hour later, when I returned to apologize, David was sitting in our bed. He looked strange. Like his skin was puffed up with air, making his entire body appear larger than normal. His breath was shallow.

"Are you okay?" I asked.

"Yelling is not okay with me," he said, slowly. "It's not okay with me to have yelling in this relationship. Yelling is off the table."

"Um, okay."

I was startled by David's intensity. Yet it seemed like a reasonable request and a good habit. So after that, we never yelled at one another.

That didn't mean I was quiet. I would get animated, talk loudly, and wave my hands. I would occasionally shout *about* a topic. But I would never shout *at* David. We didn't call each other names or fling insults at one another. We fought fairly. We used I-statements and validated one another's feelings and perspectives, even when we vehemently disagreed about a topic. We didn't hide our difficult emotions, but for the most part we processed conflict skillfully.

So when David told me his decision about Alyana, I had to flee.

After Michaela called, we agreed we wouldn't talk about it until the morning. We agreed we both needed time to think.

In the morning, David got up and took a long walk. I lay in bed, allowing myself to consider what I really wanted. When I did, I couldn't deny the truth—I wanted Alyana back. I wanted to adopt her. I knew it would be hard. I knew she could be a tough kid, and things might only get more difficult as she grew older. I knew she might implode during adolescence. I knew it would mean sacrificing our peace and quiet, probably for years. But I wanted her. I loved her. And unlike David, I wanted the lifestyle that came with having a bigger family. I wanted to stand on the sidelines at the playground with other parents, watching the kids climb and spin and slide. I wanted the back-and-forth between bedrooms at night, saying prayers and giving backrubs to two girls. I wanted the hectic, exhausting, lively juggle of family life. I wanted Alyana, and I wanted to be her mother again.

Yet I had made an explicit agreement with David at the beginning of this journey that we wouldn't adopt. So it seemed like he should get to voice his opinion first. He should have veto power. I was nervous about what he would say, but I thought back to our conversation in October. He had said then that he would be willing to adopt Alyana.

David didn't return for a long time. I texted him mid-morning, and he said he had walked to the bookstore and gotten a cup of coffee. He would be back in twenty minutes. I drove Lila to a friend's house and dropped her off. When I got back, David was there.

"Do you want to talk about it?" I said.

"Okay."

"Well, I think you should go first. We made an agreement at the beginning, and I think you should have the veto vote about whether we adopt her or not." My voice was quiet but steady.

"Okay, that's nice. Thank you." David inhaled. "I don't want to do it, Kate. I don't want to adopt her. I just can't commit to parenting for the next twenty years. I am fifty-five years old. I just can't do it. I'm not prepared to sign up for this. I love Alyana, but I don't feel called to parent her permanently."

I was quiet. I had made a commitment to myself not to react quickly, whatever he said.

"I just want to clarify something," I said. "A few months ago, you said that you'd be willing to adopt her."

David sighed and rubbed his hands together. "Yes, I know. And I'm sorry I wavered that day. I was caught by surprise. But now I've had a few months to think about it. And back in October, I was imagining the worst—that Alyana would be placed with some marginal relative. But Michaela said that they have lots of great couples on the list who are ready to adopt."

"Okay, I hear you." I took a deep breath. "Well, it seems important that I tell you how I feel, what I really want." I paused.

Once the words were out, the divide would be cemented. We wouldn't be able to pretend that maybe there could be a happy compromise. I knew the weight of my words could cause an indelible rift between us. I knew that even if David didn't experience it, I likely always would.

"I want to adopt her."

We talked for two hours. It was clear there was no argument or point I could make that would change David's mind. He was sad and sorry.

"Well, it sounds like the decision has been made," I said icily.

"I love you. I'm so sorry this is so hard." He put his hand on my leg.

"We need to leave to go pick up Lila," I said.

"Okay, I'll go do it." He left.

The rest of the day, we kept busy. I went to the grocery store, and we watched a movie—a comedy—that night. I went to bed before David, but I couldn't sleep. At one o'clock in the morning, I began to thrash beneath the sheets.

David reached for me. "Are you okay?"

"No, I am not okay," I yelled. I bolted upright in bed, pulling the sheets off of David's chest as I moved upward. "I can't believe you're doing this! I have to leave!" I slammed the door as I left, and spent the rest of the night in the guest room.

I had no idea what to do. Even though I wanted to remain respectful and constructive in my discussions with David, there was a volcano in me that felt ready to erupt.

* * *

I got the text from David while I was at work. It was Tuesday afternoon. He had spoken to Michaela the previous day and told her about his decision. After I stormed off in the middle of the night, we had several more intense and difficult discussions. I regained my composure, and over several conversations I explained again and again why I wanted Alyana back. But David remained resolute; he loved Alyana, but he just couldn't commit to parenting her into his mid-seventies. Listening to him, I knew that nothing was going to change his mind. So I told David he could contact Michaela to tell her what he had decided. He called her Monday morning. Michaela was affirming and kind, he reported back. He told her how upset I was, and she asked him to let me know she was thinking of me.

The next day, in the middle of the afternoon, the text from David came in. "Good news! I talked to Michaela again. They found a couple to adopt the kids. She described them to me. She's a doctor and he's a teacher. They sound fabulous!"

I stared at the phone, disbelieving. I couldn't believe David was sending me this news so nonchalantly and cheerfully. Didn't he have any idea how I would react?

I pushed my chair away from my desk. In the nine years I had been at my organization, I had never left work unexpectedly in the middle of the day, except for a few times when I had gotten calls that Lila was sick. But without hesitating, I retrieved my coat and purse. I needed to get out of there. I drove out of the parking garage with tears blurring my vision, not sure where I was heading. I pulled into a gas station and went inside the store. I bought a king-sized bag of Twizzlers, a pack of cigarettes, and a bottle of water. I paid and went out to pump gas. While I was holding the nozzle, a woman pulled her car over to me.

"Excuse me. I hate to ask you this, but I'm out of work and we don't have any milk at home for the kids. Would you be able to buy us some?

I looked at her. She was driving a nice car; she didn't fit my stereotype of someone who would be asking for a handout. But I nodded. "Okay, sure. Do you need anything else?"

"Well, if you don't mind, I could really use some gas, too."

I nodded. "Okay. You can fill it up." I swiped my card at her station.

"Oh, thank you so much." She got out of her car. As she got closer to me, she saw the tears on my cheeks. "Oh, honey. Are you okay?"

I shook my head. "No, not really."

"Is somebody sick? Is your family okay?"

"It's complicated. Hard to explain."

She reached toward me. "Come here." She gave me a long hug. "I'm so sorry, whatever it is."

I leaned into her, feeling the reciprocity of how we were both ministering to one another in that moment.

"Thank you." I went back in the store and bought her a gallon of whole milk.

When I got outside, I handed it to her and we hugged again.

"Thank you so much," she said.

"Thank you. Take care."

We each drove away. I headed to the playground where we used to take Alyana, and parked my car. I ate my Twizzlers and lit a cigarette.

13
Online Profile

I MADE THE MISTAKE OF GOOGLING the woman who had agreed to adopt Alyana. It had been a week since Michaela had given us the news. The day I left work, David arranged childcare for Lila and we met for dinner. As we ate our burgers, I could barely speak to him or look him in the eye. When I spoke, my words were laced with fury. I had never in my life been this angry. He didn't understand why I was so upset. I knew he was going to call Michaela. We had discussed it and agreed on the plan. And they had selected a fabulous couple who lived nearby. They had made it clear to the couple, Joan and Keith, that the vision was that we would stay in Alyana's life. David knew I was sad and still upset with him, but he didn't understand why the text messages about Joan and Keith had made me so angry. Wasn't I glad that Alyana would have good people as parents?

I tried to explain to him the depth of my jealousy. There was another woman out there—a woman just a few miles away—who would get to be Alyana's mother. It was difficult to put the intensity of my feelings into words.

A few days later, Michaela sent us Joan and Keith's contact information and asked if we would be willing to schedule a call with them sometime to talk about Alyana. Joan and Keith would have their first visit with the kids that weekend, and they were eager to learn as much about them as they could. I told David I wasn't ready. There was no way that I was ready to talk with them.

I retreated into my room, where I Googled Joan's name on my laptop. I read a few paragraphs and snapped the screen shut. Seeing her picture and reading about her just made it worse. She was pretty and accomplished. She was a successful and well-respected physician; her medical practice had five-star reviews from all her patients.

I knew my anger and jealousy at this person I had never met was beyond irrational. Of all the adults in the situation—Candace, Jacqueline, David, me—Joan and Keith were the only people who were wholly innocent. They were the only people who did not deserve an ounce of my anger. And I didn't know anything about them or their story. Yet all of my fury turned toward them. I picked up my journal and began a letter to Joan. It was a letter I never intended to send, but in it I poured out all my rage and grief.

I hate this situation more than I can possibly say. I hate that you get to have the thing I've longed to have for so long. The thing that was almost within my grasp, but now is being taken away. Alyana, this little person, my girl, will literally be yours. I hate that David's immediate and unquestioning instinct is to love you. To be your ally and your friend. His instinct is even to be family with you. I hate, hate, hate that after all the emotional work I've done to let go, to accept Alyana's departure, to love David despite our differences—I hate (times a thousand) that I still have more work to do. Huge work. I have to find a way to love you, accept you, be kind to you, support you, befriend you. I hate and utterly cannot believe that I have to do these things.

My hand kept moving, filling page after page. As I wrote, I slowly became calmer and more rational, but not by much. I took a deep breath, wondering if and how I could rely on Christian principles as the intensity of emotion threatened to overwhelm me. I figured I should ask myself, *What would Jesus do?*

But instead of Jesus, I kept thinking about Pharaoh in the book of Exodus in the Old Testament. That week in church, we had read a passage about Moses' negotiations with Pharaoh to let the enslaved Israelites go free. Pharaoh's reaction had made me laugh. Who could have possibly refused Moses' multiple requests for freedom after facing God's seven plagues? Blood in the Nile, swarms of frogs and gnats, boils on the humans and animals, hail and thunder, locusts, darkness and death. Still, Pharaoh's heart remained hardened (Exodus 7-11). I snickered while reading it. I felt like Pharaoh. I wrote about him in my letter to Joan. And I also wrote about the woman, a sinner, in the New Testament, whom we had also read about that week:

> *The New Testament speaks of the ministry of reconciliation. Of forgiveness and love. This week, I read about the woman who kissed Jesus' feet and anointed him with precious, expensive, perfumed oil. She turned herself over to God and asked for God's mercy, and she was forgiven. She was so thankful and in love with the Lord that she washed his feet with her tears and wiped them with her own hair. I admire that woman, and I want to be like her. But I am more tempted right now to be like Pharaoh and keep my heart hardened. I would like to be able to say that I don't hate you, but I do.*

A few days before, I had read a passage in a book by Caryll Houselander, and I knew— *knew* when I read it—that the passage was meant for me. Houselander wrote about Mary's inevitable loss of Jesus in his death. Mary's experience of loving and letting go epitomized what we are all required to do as humans. Houselander wrote, "Naturally then she experienced the loss of the Child, because it is an experience we all have to go through, that our love may be sifted and purified." In my journal, I wrote another letter to Joan about this idea.

I can see that this moment is a chance for my love for Alyana to become purified. A moment when my egoism and jealousy and anger and hurt and disbelief could burn away and be purified into something better, holier. Maybe something even more real. My love for Alyana, and maybe a love for you, Joan, could be a bigger kind of love. I could maybe love you, my neighbor, as myself. David says the Buddhist definition of love is the desire for another to be happy.

My better self knows that I do not want a hardened heart like Pharaoh's. God parted the waters of the sea for Moses, and maybe— hopefully—God will part the waters for me so I can be a little bit more like that woman with Jesus: grateful, humble, asking God for mercy, and then thanking God for God's grace.

I prayed for you a little bit this afternoon, Joan, for the first time. At the beginning, it didn't work. I kept saying no, in my heart. But I remembered that woman with the perfumed oil, and I was able to say a small prayer asking that you and Keith will be happy. I'm not sure I meant it, but let's hope I might mean it someday.

Writing Joan these letters was cathartic, so I kept doing it. Two weeks later, we had our first phone call with them, and it went well. Afterward, I wrote Joan another letter in my journal:

What constitutes a sin? Is it feelings and thoughts? Or just actions? I spoke to you and Keith today. David told me afterward that I did a good job. He said I was warm and kind. He even said I was generous. We told you stories about Alyana. We were empathetic, encouraging, reassuring. We gave you valuable information about the family. It felt like we developed rapport.

So does my lingering hatred for you qualify as a sin?

I stalked a woman in the grocery store this weekend, wondering if it was you. I followed her around the produce and meat aisles. She had blond hair like you do in the picture I saw online. When she was checking out, I circled the cashier station, trying to get a glimpse of the name on the credit card. Finally, I asked the woman, "Are you Joan?"

"No," the stranger replied, smiling, surprised. "I'm Laura. Why? Did you think I was someone you know?

Adrenaline had flooded my body. My heart was pounding, and I felt tears pricking my eyes. "Oh, yes, sorry. I thought you might be someone I've been looking for."

Looking for. I've been looking for you for the past three weeks. Everywhere I go, I'm looking for you. When we finally meet in person, what will you be like? Perky? Down-to-earth? Annoying? Appealing?

Your existence drives me to the brink of jealous madness. While I was able to keep my composure on the call today, I also felt like clawing my own cheeks. I know it's melodramatic, but I feel like I have a belly full of black snakes. They're in me, squirming in a twisted pile.

I'm still so sad and raw, but David is hoping we can move on. He's ready, and he wants to embrace you and Keith. But he also admitted today, after we talked to you, that he felt some jealousy, too. Jealous that he will be displaced by Keith. Is it a sin that his jealousy gives me a twisted sense of pleasure and gratification?

Lila is calling me. She wants to go outside together to make a fairy house in the yard. Is it a sin that I don't appreciate enough what I already have? That for a decade, I have yearned for more? Lila is like the most delicious piece of chocolate cake, and ever since she's been born I've wanted another slice. Is that craving a sin? Is it a sin that I've spent Lila's childhood being distractedly tied up in knots about something it turns out I'll never have?

Yeah, that seems like a sin.

That week at church, a guest preacher, Stanley Hauer-was, the well-known theologian from Duke University, talked about sin. In his sermon, he said, "Sin isn't what we do. It is what possesses us."

As I heard his words, I thought about my cousin who had given birth to a baby boy earlier that summer. For years, I had been possessed by a jealously of all the women around me who had—and kept having—babies. In the days preceding the birth of my cousin's son, I struggled again with my demons. Then, when the doctors were worried about signs of a potential heart defect that had shown up on the prenatal tests, I swung into pious, prayerful concern. After the baby was born, it turned out that, thankfully, he was fine. And I was horrified to watch, as if in slow motion, the dark thoughts of jealousy and resentment that crowded back, threatening to overshadow my relief and gratitude.

In the fog of self-recrimination that followed, the light that helped illuminate the way forward came from gazing at the photograph of my cousin's baby, taken just moments after he was born, while he was still on the hospital warming table. His beautiful baby skin was a shiny beacon. His pink body glowed like a little red pepper, and his eyelids glistened with the ointment that the hospital puts into newborns' eyes. Perhaps it was because so many people had been praying for his safe and healthy delivery that he was particularly luminescent. I started to see that the way through my guilt and possessed sinfulness was the love I felt radiating for him. His skin was shining, and I got to bask in the glow.

I wondered if I could learn to do the same—even in a small way— with Joan and Keith.

14
Letting Go

THE DAY WE MET JOAN AND KEITH in person, I couldn't sit still. In meetings at work, I got up to "stretch my back," but really it was just that I couldn't remain in one place for longer than a few minutes. I had refused to invite "Mr. and Mrs. Fabulous"—as I'd taken to calling them—to the house for dinner, although David wanted us to invite them over. I wanted to meet on neutral ground so if I needed to make a rapid escape to the bathroom to cry or scream or have a silent panic attack, I could do so. I didn't want them at our house. I wanted more control. I wanted to be able to walk away.

So we met at a nearby pizza place for an early dinner. Keith showed up first. Joan was coming from work and would arrive separately. Handsome and athletic-looking,

Keith wore stylish sunglasses and had a thread of stubble running along his jaw.

"I'm sorry, my hands are sweaty." He wiped his palms on his jeans before grasping David's hand. "I got off of school at four o'clock, and walked here. This is my exercise for the day." He smiled warmly.

Joan arrived five minutes later. She was pretty, with short blond hair. Within a minute, I could tell that they were both great. As we sat chatting, they were clearly funny, kind, interesting, emotionally intelligent. In gentle ways, they acknowledged the difficult terrain we were all navigating. Their comments about the situation weren't heavy duty; none of us broached the more difficult topics. But everything they said demonstrated that they were insightful and caring, thoughtful and eager to do right by the kids they were welcoming into their home.

We ordered food and lemonades. Over dinner, we chatted about where we'd grown up and Lila's plans for the summer. When Lila went into the restaurant to get a cookie, Keith got up to join her, and they joked about whether oatmeal cookies should *really* be considered dessert. Keith thought the presence of both oatmeal and raisins seemed to negate the desired level of decadence of dessert. I heard Lila laughing as she followed him inside.

"We're spending every Saturday afternoon with the kids during this transition period," Joan said. "Jacqueline wants to take it slow, and we respect that. I know how hard this is for all of them." Joan's eyes suddenly filled with tears. "My heart aches for Charles, and for Jacqueline, too. I know it's tearing her up inside to let the two younger kids go."

"Yes, Jacqueline is great," I said. "We've always had a really positive connection with her."

As we ate our cookies, we talked about what we each did for a living. I explained to Keith and Joan that I had worked in public health since I graduated from college—first, leading adolescent pregnancy prevention programs for low-income youth, and now working internationally to increase access to contraception.

"So if you want me to be part of the team that has The Talk about birth control with Alyana when she gets older, I'm happy to." I smiled. "I'm well-qualified."

"Definitely," Joan said. "We're going to need all the help we can get. You can chair the sex ed committee. We'd love to delegate that to you."

We all laughed.

When we'd finished dessert, we hugged and promised to be in touch again soon.

"Let us know how we can help," David said. "We'd be happy to provide any support we can."

"Yeah," I said, "we can bring you guys dinner when the kids move in, if that would be useful."

"That would be great," Keith said. "I'm sure we'll have our hands very full. We have a lot to learn." He smiled.

They got into their car, and we waved as they pulled out of the parking lot.

Once inside our car, I leaned my head back against the seat and closed my eyes.

"You did really well." David squeezed my hand. "You were really kind. I'm proud of you."

"Yeah, well my priest always says it's a lot harder to hate your neighbor once you've met them. Now we've met them, and I can't hate them. They're great. I mean, they really are. I really like them."

I paused. "I'm just not sure that makes it any easier."

As we drove home, I reminded myself again that it *should* make it easier. If Alyana wasn't going to come back to us, *of course* it was better that she was going to Mr. and Mrs. Fabulous, rather than to a marginal home. The rational part of me knew this was true. A couple from our foster care class had been fostering Sam, a three-year old boy, for the past sixteen months, and recently the court had unexpectedly decided to return custody to his biological mother, despite the mother's history of substance abuse, chronic poverty, and domestic violence. She had finally broken up with the boyfriend who had been beating her up, and that was the step the court had been waiting for her to make. Our friends had been hoping to adopt Sam, and for a long time it looked like it was heading that way. Instead, the judge made the surprise decision that because the mother had finally shown some progress, Sam would be reunited with her as soon as she finished a two-week substance-abuse treatment program. Besides being sick with grief, my friends were paralyzed with worry for him. What kind of home would he be returning to?

So *of course* it was great that Joan and Keith were fabulous. It was great that they seemed sane and smart and caring. It was wonderful for Alyana and Kaila that they clearly had resources—financial, emotional—and according to what they'd shared at dinner—an extensive support network of family and friends. This was much more than many kids in foster care would ever hope to get.

Yeah, it was great. I was thrilled.

Yet it felt a little like learning that your ex-husband was getting re-married to a wonderful woman. This meant that your kids would have the benefit of having a super-duper fabulous stepmom. And *of course* it was better that your kids have a super-duper fabulous stepmom rather than a crappy one. I mean, any rational person would want that. Right?

Part of me still wanted to tell Keith to shove his stylish sunglasses up his rear end.

How do you learn to love your neighbor when you still hate them? And how do you forgive yourself for your own blatant sinfulness when you hate someone who is obviously awesome, kind, and generous?

The author and pastor Nadia Bolz-Weber speaks to these questions. In her book *Accidental Saints*, she explains that while we celebrate the lives of saints in the church, the distinction between sinners and saints becomes blurry quickly. She writes, "When Jesus again and again says things like the last shall be first, and the first shall be last, and the poor are blessed, and the rich are cursed, and that prostitutes make great dinner guests, it makes me wonder if our need for pure black-and-white categories is not true religion, but maybe actually a sin." She goes on to say, "It has been my experience that what makes us the saints of God is not our ability to be saintly, but rather God's ability to work through sinners....We believe in a God who gets redemptive and holy things done in this world through, of all things, human beings, all of whom are flawed."

So even though I was clearly flawed, all I could hope was that something holy and redemptive was going to come out of all of this. And the truth was, now that I had met Joan and Keith in person, I could feel my jealousy and irrational anger starting to dissipate. After meeting them, I already liked them, so maybe I could even grow to love them.

That day, I wasn't sure what loving Joan and Keith would involve. I imagined it would include offering support and friendship and tangible help. But the months ahead would reveal something I wasn't expecting: that loving Keith and Joan, and ultimately loving Alyana as well, would require the most difficult work of all—letting them go.

15
Embargo

A FEW WEEKS BEFORE ALYANA MOVED IN with Keith and Joan, Michaela informed us that we needed to wait at least eight weeks before we visited her. David and I were caught off guard. Over the summer, Michaela and Deborah, the therapist, as well as Keith and Joan, had all reiterated that they wanted us to stay in Alyana's life. They agreed that another abandonment would not be good for her. But Michaela explained in an email that Deborah also felt that Alyana needed a "nesting period," and that contact with us could potentially be disruptive.

David and I didn't understand. If the therapist wanted Alyana to avoid feeling abandoned, wasn't this the especially vulnerable period when having consistent contact could help normalize and contextualize things for her?

When Alyana moved in with Jacqueline, there hadn't been any break in contact. Why the difference? Our instinct was to stop by Joan and Keith's condo at least once before the "nesting period" began. We thought it would be good to bring them dinner, celebrate Alyana's new house, room, dog, toys. Give her our implicit and explicit blessing.

But now, unexpectedly, we were being treated as though our presence had the potential to be disruptive and threatening. Suddenly, after being on the other side of things for a year, it felt like we were a factor that needed to be carefully managed.

I spent the next few weeks looking over my shoulder everywhere I went—the grocery store, CVS, restaurants, the library. We had bumped into Candace multiple times when Alyana was with us, and it seemed inevitable that in a small town we would at some point cross paths with Keith and Joan. Every time I left the house, I was braced for an unexpected encounter.

But when the encounter did happen, it wasn't what I had anticipated. I wasn't even there. Lila bumped into them on her own.

Lila was out with a friend's family at a local puppet show. Afterward, as the crowd moved slowly toward the exit, Lila was suddenly face-to-face with Alyana. She told me later that Alyana had yelped with joy, and the girls hugged each other fiercely. But the moment was over quickly. I never found out how they parted, if Joan and Keith called Alyana away, or if she scampered off on her own.

Afterward, Lila was inconsolable. She cried that night,

and then every day that week. One evening at bedtime, she wailed, "I don't understand! Why can't I see her? Why did they put an embargo on us?"

My throat tightened. I didn't know Lila knew that word. *Embargo* sounded too grown-up coming out of her mouth. I guess she'd been listening to our hushed grumblings over the past few weeks.

I rubbed her back. "It's okay, honey. Don't worry. We're going to see her soon."

Only ten more days, and then the waiting period would be over. We emailed Michaela and got the green light. She said we should keep it brief and meet on neutral ground. She included Joan and Keith on the email, and they suggested we meet for ice cream.

That Sunday, we arrived first. When Joan and Keith pulled in and unstrapped Alyana from her car seat, she ran across the yard to us and David lifted her up.

"Daddy!" She squeezed his neck.

David gave Alyana a hug, and then shook Keith's hand. Joan was holding Kaila, who had grown bigger in the two months since we'd last seen her. But Alyana looked the same.

"I want a chocolate ice cream!" Alyana reached for me, and I took her from David.

I squeezed her. "Okay, let's go into the store with your family," I said, keeping my voice cheerful. "I wonder what kind of ice cream your mom and dad want to get."

Before the meeting, I had been unsure how to refer to Joan and Keith, but now it seemed obvious that we should reinforce their role as the parents.

"Let's all go in," I said.

After we got our order, we sat on the white rocking chairs on the porch. Alyana swung her legs. She seemed content, and Lila was relaxed. I was pleased with how well things seemed to be going. The ice cream turned soupy in the heat and started to drip on Alyana's shirt.

"Come here, honey. Let me wipe you off," I said, without thinking, and then cringed.

I could feel how quickly the impulse to parent Alyana rose up in me. As she and Lila ran toward the yard to play, I wanted to warn Alyana not to go too near the street. I wanted to ask her if she wanted a sip of water before she headed out into the heat of the day. I wanted to put sunscreen on her face and wipe the stickiness from her hands. But that wasn't my role anymore. None of it was essential, and I was a visitor in her life.

Keith and I chatted about how things were going, and their plans to enroll Alyana in kindergarten for the fall. Joan was giving Kaila a bottle of formula.

"How do you think Alyana's doing with the transition?" I asked Keith.

"She has good days and bad. I think it's going okay, but there are some really tough moments." He gazed at her, across the grass. "We had a tough morning with her."

I nodded. I remembered the tough moments.

Lila and Alyana ran back to the porch.

"Why don't you take a few minutes alone with her," Keith said.

I felt awkward about the idea. I wanted us all to stay together, to have it feel normal that our families would be integrated. But I smiled my assent, and Keith and Joan took Kaila inside.

"Here, Alyana. I made this for you." Lila handed her a stone she had painted at camp. It had their names and a heart in the middle.

"Thank you!" Alyana balanced the stone on the rocking chair arm. "I love this rock!"

"Maybe you can put it by your new bed, " I said. "What color is your room?"

"Yellow! And one wall is white. With star stickers."

"Oh, that sounds gorgeous."

Alyana frowned. She turned to David and stared at him. "Do you remember when you were my daddy?" Her voice was quiet and serious.

"Yes, I do remember," he said, gently.

"Now Keith is my daddy."

"That's right. Keith is your daddy. He really loves you."

Alyana nodded and picked up the rock. "I have a doggie at my new house."

"What's the doggie's name?" Lila said.

"Rosie! She has brown fur."

"Wow, that's a great name. I bet she is so cute." I hugged her. "Let's go inside and show your parents your new rock."

We went inside. It was clear that Kaila was getting fussy. Only forty minutes of our allotted hour was up, but I could tell Joan and Keith were ready to go. They nodded when we asked if it would be a good time to wrap things up.

"Okay, it's time to go," I said. "It's great to see you, Alyana. We really love you." I handed her to David, and we said our goodbyes.

She hadn't called me mommy, and she didn't cry as they pulled away in the car. It seemed like the visit had gone well. She hadn't had a meltdown, and neither had I. I was relieved for both of us.

* * *

A few days later, David wrote Keith and Joan a note to ask how things were going and how Alyana had reacted to the visit. David included the social worker, Michaela, on the email. A few hours later, we received a disturbing reply from Michaela. She explained that while the family had enjoyed seeing us, the fallout from the visit had been on the verge of devastating for Alyana. Michaela explained that since then, Alyana had been having unusually large and sustained tantrums, and she was using phrases like, "I don't have any parents," and "No one loves me." They hadn't heard her say this type of thing before.

Michaela explained that they certainly didn't blame us, but they needed to prioritize helping Alyana find a place of comfort and peace. She wrote that they couldn't commit to scheduling another visit. She suggested we check in again in another month or two.

I was standing behind David as we both read the email on his desktop computer. In unison, we inhaled sharply.

Six weeks passed, and we reached out to Michaela again. Kindergarten was starting in a few days, she explained. The team wanted Alyana to have time to settle into her new routine without the disruption another visit could cause. We understood. Another month passed. I was growing more accustomed to her absence, but Alyana was in my thoughts all the time. Six, seven, eight times a day I ran through the *what if's* in my mind. What if we'd kept her? What would that have meant for Alyana? For Lila? For David? For me? What if she was still ours?

Finally, we wrote Michaela and asked to schedule a phone call.

"Please, I need to know where this is heading," I said, on the call. "We know the original vision was for us to stay in Alyana's life. We don't need to know today, or even in the next few weeks or months. But we ultimately want to understand what role Keith and Joan envision us playing in Alyana's life. Jacqueline had said that she wanted us to be Alyana's legal godparents." I took a deep breath. "Is the vision that we're going to be like extended family, or that we'll be more like acquaintances?"

I paused, and David continued. "We realize that our presence has the potential to be both a blessing and a curse. We get why it could be disruptive. But we still think we could provide continuity and love for Alyana, and be a source of support for Keith and Joan. We had hoped to remain a substantial part of Alyana's life."

"Yes, yes. I totally understand." I heard Michaela sigh. "That was our hope, too. So this is really tough. But we need to facilitate her bond with Keith and Joan, and help her feel secure in her new home."

"We understand if a visit is too provocative at this point," I said. "What if we planned a Skype video call? That way, we could stay connected but also have some distance."

"That's an interesting suggestion. Let me talk it over with the therapist. I'll get back to you. Thanks for your patience and understanding."

We hung up.

After that, no word back. Several more weeks passed. Then one afternoon, the email came from Michaela:

Hi Kate & David,

Thank you for your patience. I was hoping to get back to you sooner. The therapist and I finally connected this week after she was out of town. The thought of the team right now is to have you as more of acquaintances than extended family. Although Alyana is making progress in so many ways, it is still daily work for her to feel secure and regulated. Kindergarten has been a hard adjustment for her and is requiring much of her whole team. We are also trying to balance contact with Jacqueline, Charles, and Candace.

All that to say, the therapist's recommendation is that contact with your family should be very limited. I'm going to be honest here in saying that this is a really tough situation for me to navigate because I know how much you love Alyana and how much she loves you. I definitely hear your point that having more frequent contact could normalize it for her. Ultimately, I am supporting the recommendation of her therapist. My hope, which I know that Joan and Keith share, is that as Alyana bonds with them, feels more secure, and grows up, she can more easily voice her feelings about what kind of contact she wants with you and that it can be more "normal."

You asked about a general timeline for contact. I think at this point it makes the most sense for me to reach out to you next. I don't want you to feel like you have to guess the right time, although you are always welcome to contact me. I will be in touch at the beginning of next year unless something significant changes before then.

Many thanks,

Michaela

That was it. I turned away from the computer screen. The embargo would continue. Indefinitely.

16

Acquiescence

THREE YEARS BEFORE ALYANA WAS PLACED with us—before David and I had even seriously considered the possibility of becoming foster parents, and instead were caught in an endless struggle about whether to have another baby—I sought counsel during a one-on-one meeting with the priest at my church. I told him that I knew I had to make peace with David's decision that he didn't want another child, but I couldn't seem to find any sense of resolution. I couldn't stop fighting it. I had asked God a dozen different ways, and I seemed to be getting the same answer over and over in my prayers. I had the clear sense that God didn't intend us to have another biological baby, that God had something else in mind for us. But despite this,

I kept fighting the response I received. Fighting against acceptance. Asking God, like God was an uncooperative game show contestant, "Is that *really* your final answer?" Occasionally, I found resolution, but then I would snatch my resistance back, clutching it to my chest indignantly, still taken aback that it didn't seem like I was going to get my way.

During our meeting, my priest looked at me kindly. He took a breath. Nodding, he laid a hand on my shoulder.

"Maybe it's time to acquiesce."

No one had ever said that to me before.

* * *

Acquiescence is a different word than surrender. For me, the word surrender has always held a certain lightness. Surrender is a letting go. It's setting a bottle that contains a message to God, with your deepest secrets, fears, and desires, out on an ocean wave and allowing it to float away. It's letting all of your resistance, ego, and pride blow away like dandelion fuzz in an afternoon breeze.

To acquiesce feels like an earthier, heavier process. It's less of a letting go, and more of a giving in. It's bowing down, literally and figuratively, until your forehead touches the floor. And then it's going down even further still, until your whole body is spread out, with your cheek resting on the cool tile. It's a laying down of arms so fully that you're assuming a posture both of complete humility and complete trust. And it is in that full body release that something new emerges—relief. With a cheek on the floor, you're finally able to give up the fight. To rest in the release.

* * *

When Alyana was with us, I constantly experienced the difference between being a foster parent and a biological parent. When I would give Alyana a bath, I would reach in to wash her hair from outside the stall, trying not to get splashed as I turned her sudsy hair into a tall point on the top of her head. A few times, it would have been more practical to take her into the shower with me. Times when we both needed to bathe and there was time pressure to get the task done. But in those moments, I wasn't sure what the rules dictated. When it was my own child, I never gave a second thought about whether it was appropriate to take a two- or three-year-old girl into the shower with me. Lila and I had occasionally showered together when she was a young child. But Alyana was a ward of the state. Was there an explicit set of guidelines about nudity in a manual somewhere that I had failed to read?

This was the uncertainty and constant low-grade anxiety that hung on me as a foster parent. I could always feel the eyes of the state on us—waiting with the potential to condemn or question. What if Alyana got hurt? What if the scrapes on her leg and arms were questioned by her teacher or the pediatrician? When Alyana first came to us with a bad diaper rash, a long-time, experienced foster parent had advised us to take photographs so that there would be documentation it hadn't happened on our watch. This was the opposite experience I had after Lila was born.

"Isn't there someone we're supposed to call?" I asked, a few weeks after Lila's birth, when we were struggling with a mundane question about sleep and eating schedules. "I mean, isn't there someone in *charge*?"

The deafening silence in that moment is shocking to all new parents. *You* are in charge. Without any certification or training or oversight, you have to make the tough calls and the hard, murky choices about what to do with this precious human life. As Lila's parents, David and I didn't report to anyone; we were floundering, mostly alone. When you're a foster parent, it's the opposite. Decisions are made by "the team." You have to send updates, schedule home visits, consult with multiple professionals. Sometimes if feels comforting to have the back-up. Sometimes it feels like common sense gets lost in the process. Sometimes you don't want to ask what "the team" thinks.

So when Alyana was with us, I didn't take her into the shower with me, as I would have done with my own child. Instead, I stayed outside the tub, leaning forward to reach into her. After her bath, I would lift her out of the water and carry her across the room to the sink. In those moments, she would lean against me, head on my shoulder, her hair a wet, heavy blanket across her back. Looking at our reflection in the mirror, I would close my eyes for a moment. Despite all the stresses and uncertainties, in that moment, there was no distinction between foster child and biological child. There was only love. My mind was quiet as I toweled the water out of Alyana's hair.

* * *

If acquiescence means giving up, I didn't do it after my priest gave me the advice. I didn't lie down; I didn't put my face against the floor. I kept fighting for what I wanted. I wanted more parenting, a bigger family, another sweet child in my arms. I had fought for it—and briefly, I had gotten it. Now that Alyana was gone, the priest's advice came back to me. I knew that the only way forward was to let go. I could feel, at the deepest level, the futility of continuing to fight. I was at the end of the line. Alyana wasn't ours. It was over, and we had lost her.

I've only ever heard one definition of forgiveness that made any sense to me. A workshop leader told me that forgiveness is acknowledging the space between the life you wanted and the life you have, and making peace with that gap in between. The fight with David over whether to have another child, the loss of Alyana—these had become the defining struggles of my adulthood. And now it felt clear that accepting the gap in my life and letting go—of the remorse, the anger, the resentment—this was the central challenge that remained.

The fall that Alyana started kindergarten, I gave a talk about my religious journey and my writing to a mostly secular group in my community. There was a woman about my age in the audience. She was clearly angry at organized religion in general, and Christianity most acutely. I could tell she was trying to be polite, but her comments were difficult and pointed. At the end of my talk, she inhaled sharply. On the exhale, she tried to regain her composure.

"I do have a final question I'd like to ask. Do you feel like Christianity asks you to give up your agency? And if so, doesn't that bother you?"

I contemplated her question for weeks. Yes, of course Christianity asks me to give up my agency, I wanted to tell her, after the class was over and it was too late to reply. That's the whole point, the whole beauty and blessing and power of being a disciple of Christ and devoting my life to God. The hope is that if I can let go of my ironclad grip on my ego, pride, and desires, perhaps I can start to discern and follow God's will.

Jesus said to Peter, "When you were younger, you used to fasten your own belt and to go wherever you wished. But when you grow old, you will stretch out your hands and someone else will fasten a belt around you and take you where you do not wish to go" (John 21: 18). It always amazes me how Jesus' words—infused with the promise of something that seems so inherently dissonant, with how we typically structure our entire lives—feel so compelling and so right. And his command clearly requires acquiescence.

So now, as we faced the possibility that we might not be allowed to have any relationship with Alyana at all, what was God asking of me? How could this be more than just a moment of beaten-down resignation and grief? Could I avoid more anger? What would it mean to acquiesce? I loved Alyana with a passionate fury. I loved her with my whole heart. What was I supposed to do with that?

"It feels like it was all a mistake," I complained to David. We were sitting on the balcony with beers and a box of Kleenex, talking about Michaela's email. "I shouldn't have loved Alyana so ferociously. It's just made it harder on her and on me."

"I think," David said, quietly. "I think this is an opportunity. You can keep loving her. But it is with a love that is not possessive."

I was silent, thinking about his words. Could the task at hand be learning to love without needing to possess or hold on? This sounded like a spiritual superpower, unattainable for any normal mortal. Could I simultaneously love Alyana with ferocity *and* let her go? I wasn't sure, but it was an intriguing possibility.

And if this was God's will that I learn to love and to let go, where else would that call lead?

17

A Quiet Life

I AM MARRIED TO A QUIET MAN. I gave birth to a quiet daughter. In most ways, David and Lila are temperamentally similar to one another. They would rather be at home, reading on the couch, than doing almost anything else. Going to a party is, at best, unappealing. At worst, it is emotionally exhausting and alienating for both of them.

I am the opposite. I am decidedly not quiet. I hunger for social contact, emotional stimulation, meaningful and fun interactions. I desire intimate, intense, one-on-one conversations, and loud, animated discussions in large groups. I like to organize people and events; just the act of organizing them is, in itself, a recreational activity for me.

In the year after Alyana left, one of the things I missed most about her was her companionship and willingness to venture out into the world with me. Even more than me, she was inexhaustibly social. She was always ready to meet a new person, join in an activity, tag along on an errand. David and Lila often declined to join us. Once, I took Alyana to a co-worker's house for a bonfire party. She was excited to join me; David and Lila had opted to stay at home. Within ten minutes of arriving, Alyana had run off with three pre-teen girls to jump on the trampoline in the backyard. Alyana made friends easily and without reserve. We all worried about this to a certain degree. Her willingness to connect to any stranger, ready to talk or play—or even to wander off with them, if given the chance—seemed symptomatic of at least a mild attachment disorder. What would this quality translate into as she got older, particularly in her romantic relationships?

But as a three-year-old, she was a fun and well-suited companion for me.

With her gone, even after a year, the house still felt too quiet. When Alyana was with us, we planned back-to-back activities to have a vehicle to channel her endless energy. With David and Lila, it would take twenty minutes of cajoling to convince them to take a walk around the block with me after dinner. As a family of three, I found that, energetically, I was often out of sync with their rhythm. I craved a different type of engagement with the wider world than the two people with whom I spent the majority of my time.

I didn't know what to do with this disconnect. I had to make peace with Alyana's absence in so many ways.

Beyond letting go of my anger at David and the grief at what could have been, I had to shake the low-grade dissatisfaction with the prevailing quiet in our home.

A few weeks after we got Michaela's email, I went on a long jog in the woods near our house. I was a late-to-life jogger, and my pace was incredibly slow. Whenever I could convince Lila to accompany me, she would walk briskly at my side, easily keeping up while I huffed along. She teased me endlessly about this. I would laugh and agree with her assessment of my sluggishness.

Normally, I made a slow loop around my neighborhood, but that day, I drove twenty minutes and jogged on a forest trail. Tall, dark tree trunks lined the path, with an awning of vibrant green leaves overhead. I didn't see another person the entire time. I felt quiet. The compulsivity that had sat with me all week, the rumination about unfinished tasks, the impulse to check my phone every four minutes, dissipated as my feet landed heavily on the earth.

I know the downside of my decidedly not-quiet life is that I can easily become frazzled and unbalanced. My constant motion and sociability often leave me feeling amped up, anxious, and over-extended. In those moments, I frequently think about an observation Henri Nouwen once made. He wrote that many of us aren't "rest-filled people who occasionally become restless. We are restless people who sometimes find rest." In the year since Alyana had left, I had been chewing on my resentment about David's insistence on a quiet lifestyle. But the truth was, I knew I needed quiet time as an antidote to my own restlessness, and David's rhythm invites me into a slower pace. We balance one another. My sociability leads to relationships and vibrancy he might not otherwise have; his tranquility helps center me.

At the end of my jog, I saw a hawk perched on a tree branch in front of me. I stopped to watch him and slowly lowered myself until I was sitting on the trail. He lifted from the branch, and I saw a small, dark form clutched in his talons. He silently flew away.

I imagined what Joan and Keith were doing that day. I knew if Alyana was with us, there likely wouldn't be time or space for me to take a leisurely jog in the woods. David and Lila wouldn't have many opportunities to read quietly on the couch without interruption. Instead, our house and lives would inevitably have been chaotic.

Once, when my mother and I were negotiating holiday plans, she texted me, "I love family bedlam!" In contrast, I know David hates commotion and disorder; this is part of why he didn't want a larger family.

I am torn. I want both—bedlam and peace. Love-filled chaos is what I am attracted to and what I also know can be enervating. I want balance, although I'm never sure how to achieve it.

All I knew was that with Alyana truly gone, the balance felt off. The house was too quiet.

18

Sisters

THE IRONY OF MY DECADE-LONG STRUGGLE with wanting another child is that I've spent my career trying to help other people keep from getting pregnant. Before I worked internationally, I worked locally, running a teen pregnancy prevention program for middle school girls living in public housing. The non-profit where I worked received an early intervention grant from the state to provide comprehensive support to at-risk girls. I led afterschool health education sessions for the participants that focused partly on contraception and STI prevention, and also on communication skills, decision-making, self-esteem, and financial literacy. The curriculum intentionally focused on much more than sex, but nevertheless, our overarching objective was clear: we wanted to help the girls avoid early, unplanned pregnancies.

My favorite participants in the program were two sisters. They had been taken away from their mother by Social Services when they were in elementary school because of her substance abuse, prostitution, and neglect. The girls had different fathers, and the older sister, Shawna, was placed in foster care, while the younger one, Keisha, went to her biological father's house. But they went to the same school and saw each other frequently.

When Shawna was in eighth grade, in her last semester of my program, I got a call from her school social worker. Shawna had a miscarriage in the school bathroom earlier that day. Nobody had known she was pregnant until she told one of her friends to get the school nurse. She was home now; she had seen a doctor and was fine. The social worker just wanted to let me know.

Shawna graduated from middle school that spring, which meant she was no longer eligible for my program. Six months later, when she was in her first semester of ninth grade, I heard from Keisha that Shawna had gotten pregnant again. She moved into a new foster home that was willing to keep her and the baby while Shawna continued to attend high school classes.

Meanwhile, Keisha seemed to be doing well. She was a quiet girl with round cheeks, who rarely spoke during activities, but seemed to have the respect of the other group members. I appreciated her intelligence and sweetness. She wrote a poem in sixth grade that concluded, "Makeup and small sizes don't make you beautiful/ Being yourself is even more wonderful/ Let this lesson be taught to those wanna-be models/ Inner beauty is the way to succeed 'til tomorrow." We submitted the poem to the local newspaper, and they published it in the community interest section.

I also liked Keisha's father. I knew all the parents of the girls in the program, and her father struck me as one of the best. He seemed stable and attentive. Keisha lived with him, his wife, and her two half-brothers.

Then, when Keisha was in the eighth grade, she disappeared. I had been hearing complaints from her over the previous six months; she said her father was too rigid and controlling. His rules and expectations were unreasonable. And Keisha seemed different; her demeanor seemed more aloof rather than shy and sweet. Her body changed, too, the softness in her cheeks gone, replaced with sharper angles in her face. And then one day, she was gone. Her father was frantic. He went to the police station and contacted family and friends. Nothing. The police were looking, but they were sure she had run away. Two weeks went by. I was distraught and went by their house every few days to see if there was any news and if there was anything I could do to help.

At this point, this had become far more than a day job for me; I cared deeply about this family. I went by the police station to see if I could push them to do more. They told me they were working on it. I saw posters of missing girls hanging in the reception area and wondered if they would make one for Keisha soon.

Then one morning, I got a call from her father. "She's

fine. I found out where she is." He sounded tired but relieved.

"What? Where?"

"She's in Durham. She's living with her boyfriend. I didn't even know she had a boyfriend."

Neither did I.

Keisha had sent word through an aunt that she was safe, but she didn't want to see or talk with her father or with me. I couldn't understand it. A few days later, her father got hold of her boyfriend's cell phone number, and he gave me the number. I tried calling her one day, but she hung up on me.

I was devastated. I reminded myself that this was just a job, and I had to let it go. But I couldn't move on. I thought about her all the time. What had happened? Why had she run away? Why didn't she want any contact with me?

Then eight months later, I got a call from Keisha's father. She was back, and they were at the hospital. It turned out that she had run away because she was pregnant and she hadn't wanted her father to know. She had shown up three days before her due date, and now she was in labor. She would likely give birth later that day.

A week later, I stopped by the apartment to drop off a bag of hand-me-down baby clothes a co-worker had donated. Keisha stood in the doorway of her father's apartment. She thanked me and turned her body sideways so I could see the baby, asleep in a bassinet. I cooed, but she didn't invite me in. I told her that she could always call me if she needed anything, and she nodded. It was summer; she was now too old to be eligible for my program. Her dad had contacted Social Services, and they would provide them both with support so, hopefully, Keisha could return to school in the fall. I gave her a small, awkward hug as I was leaving.

"Congratulations."

"Thanks."

And that was it. I tried calling a few times over the next month, but her dad answered and said that Keisha didn't want to talk. She was no longer in my program, and the boundaries were starting to feel too muddy. I stopped calling. After that, I didn't see anyone in the family for five years.

Until Lila's first day of kindergarten.

That morning, I was nervous and teary. My baby was growing up, and I worried about the transition to a large public school after the small, nurturing, half-day preschool she had attended. When we arrived, I parked my car and walked her inside, making her stop in front of the building so I could take a photograph of her wearing her blue backpack. As we entered and turned the corner into the kindergarten hallway, there was Shawna standing in the doorway.

"Hi, Kate." She sounded unsurprised to see me.

I looked at her, disoriented. "Shawna? What—what are you doing here?"

She looked at ease, like she belonged there. I did the calculation. She must have graduated from high school by then. Maybe she was working at the school. Could she be a teacher's aide? Was she working in Lila's classroom?

"My son goes here," she said. "He's in your daughter's class. We got here ten minutes ago, and I saw your name on the list."

"Your son is in this class?" My thoughts felt slow and thick. It had been awhile since I had thought about Shawna or Keisha. I had never considered that Shawna's pregnancy occurred around the same time as my own did. The moment felt surreal. Our kids would be classmates.

"Oh, wow. What a surprise."

"There he is. His name is Gabriel." Shawna pointed out a boy in red pants, sitting on the rug near the front of the room.

"Wow," I said again. "He's so big. What a cute guy."

"Yeah, he's all right." She smiled. "Your daughter's real grown up, too."

"Yeah, it's hard to believe. So what are you up to these days?" I said, regaining some of my composure.

"I cut hair. Right up the road in the shopping center. At Supercuts. Gabriel and I live about a mile from here."

"Oh, cool. That's great. And how's your sister? Are you guys in touch?"

"Oh, yeah, she's doing good. She's got a job at a nursing home. She really likes it. And she had another baby a year ago."

"Wow, another baby."

"Yeah, a second boy. It's kinda crazy, you know. But she's doing good." Shawna smiled again.

Lila tugged on my arm.

I looked down at her. "Oh, listen, I should go. I promised to help her get settled. It's a big day."

"Yeah, no problem. It's good to see you. I'm sure I'll see you again soon."

Shawna seemed relaxed and poised, but I still felt rattled.

"Have a good first day." She looked down at Lila.

Lila didn't respond, her eyes wide as she stared into the classroom.

* * *

It was uncanny. Throughout Lila's six years in elementary school, she and Gabriel ended up in the same classroom every year. On the first day of school each August, I would see his name on the list by the classroom door. Their placement together gave me the chance to observe him unobtrusively over the years. I did so with an acute awareness that I had spent thousands of taxpayer dollars trying to prevent his life. The whole thing felt bizarre to me.

I tried to reach out to him during my occasional classroom visits. I told him I knew his mom and his aunt. He would look at me briefly, not answering, and then would run off to play with his friends. But this was not unusual. Lila wasn't good at making small talk with adults either.

Once, I chaperoned a class field trip. We went to a nature reserve to take a hike and learn about local ecosystems. During the lunch break, Gabriel was required to finish some worksheets at the picnic table while the other kids ran around, playing and shouting. He scowled, his head bent over the paper, while his teacher hovered over him. I didn't know if the assignment in this unlikely setting was a consequence of a behavior issue, or a result of unfinished academic work. Either way, it was hard for me to ignore. Every observation of Gabriel became a new data point. Would this child of an unmarried teen mom be more likely to struggle than other, more privileged kids, including my own? Would Gabriel become another statistic? These questions felt unfair to him. I knew he deserved more than to be typecast, especially when he was only in the second grade.

I experienced the same push-and-pull regarding expectations for Alyana when she was with us. Whenever Alyana had an emotional outburst, it was easy to attribute her behavior to her disadvantaged background. In contrast, when Lila was small, she had terrible tantrums, but we never thought much of it. Furious if some small aspect of life was not to her liking, her outbursts were unpredictable and extreme. She would become nearly untethered, screaming and writhing on the floor. The behavior was exasperating, but we figured she would grow out of it. And she did. Now, Lila bears no resemblance to that screaming wraith who used to inhabit her toddler body.

But with Alyana's emotional outbursts, my parents and friends would nod, knowingly. "Well, after all she's been through, you have to expect it."

I saw the danger in this. I imagined that adults in her

life would begin to communicate their expectations in subtle and overt ways to Alyana, and she would begin to internalize them. Instead of being viewed as something she would naturally grow out of, Alyana's tantrums became a portend of something more sinister looming in her future. It wasn't her fault, the unspoken message seemed to be, but an explosive adolescence or adulthood was, unfortunately, most likely her destiny.

A relative gently told me that while she understood my sadness at losing Alyana, I also ought to be relieved that I would not be subjected to the terrible behavior that Alyana was sure to exhibit in the future. Her words made me furious and sad, not just because she was trying to minimize my sense of loss, but because it made me realize what an uphill battle Alyana would face to overcome others' expectations of her, and likely her own expectations of herself.

* * *

One morning, before Alyana left, I pulled into the parking lot of her daycare to drop her off. And there, standing in the parking lot of the school, was Keisha. She was helping two young boys climb out of a car. I stopped, startled, and stared at her.

The truth was, I had loved Keisha. I had been fond of Shawna, but I had truly loved Keisha. I had believed in her, rooted for her, spent extra time and effort trying to provide her with support. I cared about her more than any of the other girls in my program. Before she had run away,

I had fantasized that I would stay in her life over the long term, serving as an informal mentor and adult friend. But she hadn't wanted that. First, she fled, and then she pushed me away.

I watched her now, crossing the parking lot. Similarly to when I had first bumped into Shawna, the moment felt surreal. I hadn't seen Keisha for all these years, and now our paths were crossing because her children and my foster daughter would be schoolmates. I was almost forty, and she was eighteen years old. Yet in this way, in this space, we would be peers.

I walked into the building, holding Alyana's hand. When I got inside, there she was.

"Hey, Keisha. Hi. It's Kate."

"Hey, how are you doing?"

"Good. It's really good to see you. I've seen Shawna around. Our kids go to school together."

"Yeah, she told me."

"Did your sons just start going here?"

"Yeah, I just signed them up last week."

The moment felt awkward. Unlike with Shawna, who seemed relaxed and open during our interactions, Keisha seemed shut down. She gazed over my shoulder, and her tone was flat. She seemed disinterested, eager to move on. We chatted for about another minute, but then she nodded and drifted down the hallway. It was an unsatisfying interaction. When I had seen her outside, a fantasy had flashed through my mind. Perhaps we would reconnect and grow close again. Maybe she would explain what happened all those years ago, or confide in me how her life was going now. Maybe she would even apologize for the worry she caused when she ran away. Maybe that shy, small smile I remembered would spread across her face if we exchanged memories about good times we had spent together. But I didn't see any hint of the girl I had known, and she was gone before I could ask her how things were going for her, or even ask the names of her sons.

As Christians, we are told to love our neighbor as ourselves. Yet we do not often receive advice on how to proceed if our neighbor doesn't seem to want our love, if there is someone we love who does not or cannot love us back.

In her book about romantic relationships and Christian theology, author and pastor Bromleigh McCleneghan writes, "If you share your love with someone who cannot or does not reciprocate, it's over." Her words seem overly definitive and harsh. A relationship is definitely over if love is not reciprocated? Really? Yet McCleneghan offers some nuance by juxtaposing this intense statement with a story about Jesus feeding the five thousand. She writes that when Jesus transforms a measly five loaves of bread and two fish into enough to feed the five thousand people who have gathered around him—with enough food for leftovers— it is a "story about how trust and faith lead to abundance." Jesus' life of abundant love demonstrates that "love begets love. Kindness leads to kindness."

So maybe both of McCleneghan's points are true. Relationships may end and our love may go unreciprocated. But because God's love is abundant, love ultimately begets more love in the world. It is like the tiny mustard seed (Matthew 13:31). When it is planted in the ground, we must trust it will grow into a towering tree, even if we're not around to see it reach its fullest height or to see the birds nest in its branches.

I rarely saw Keisha after I bumped into her at Alyana's daycare that day. Our drop-off and pick-up schedules were not in sync. Later that month, I saw her again across the parking lot, but I was already pulling out of the driveway, so I didn't have a chance to say hello. A few weeks later, Alyana left our house to go to Jacqueline's. I didn't see Keisha again.

Losing Alyana also meant losing all of the expected and unexpected communities that formed around and through her. Before Alyana had gone to live with Joan and Keith, we had expected to stay in Jacqueline and Charles' lives, but now our contact with them faded to almost nothing. Jacqueline and I talked occasionally on the phone, and we commented on each other's posts on Facebook, but our monthly visits stopped. There was also the loss of regular contact with the social workers, other foster parents, Alyana's teachers and babysitters. And there was the loss of the quirky connections that emerged unexpectedly, like having contact with Keisha again after all these years.

This is a part of parenthood that we don't often think about—the ways our kids expose us to and knit us into communities we wouldn't otherwise have. And as our kids grow up and grow away, these groups change and break apart.

The June after Alyana left us, Lila and Gabriel graduated from elementary school. As we entered the auditorium for the graduation ceremony, I saw Shawna in the aisle and hugged her. She hugged me back. When Gabriel was in the fourth grade, Shawna had another child; her daughter, Reina, was now eighteen-months old. We sat next to them, and Shawna looked proud and relaxed, holding Reina on her lap. I was amazed at how different her demeanor was from Keisha's. Adult life, with two kids and a job, seemed to suit Shawna.

While we were waiting for the graduation ceremony to begin, I held Reina in my lap. She looked up at me solemnly. She had perfect, tiny features, alert eyes, and dark, tight curls. A pink band encircled her head, and she reached out to grab my glasses. I smiled and strained my neck so they were out of reach. Just then, the graduating fifth graders entered the room. Reina saw her brother and grinned, bouncing in my arms. I handed her back to her mother. Sitting side by side, Shawna and I clapped together for our children as they climbed the steps and crossed the stage. Love begets love. So all we can do is plant the seed and trust that—in ways we may never fully see or realize—our love will grow.

19

Love Made Visible

I SAT IN THE CHAIR IN THE OB/GYN'S OFFICE soon after I found out I was pregnant with Lila. I had recently taken a pregnancy test, and this was my first prenatal appointment. David had a work conflict that morning, so we had agreed I would go to the first appointment by myself and he would join for the next one. The doctor sat with me after the consultation and went over the basics: what not to eat, when to come back for check-ups, which prenatal vitamins were best.

Near the end of the appointment, she said, "Do you want me to calculate the likely conception date?"

"Sure," I replied, surprised.

It hadn't occurred to me to wonder exactly when the baby had been conceived. I told her the date of my last period, and she twisted the top layer of a paper wheel that seemed designed for this purpose.

She looked up me, smiling wryly. "Looks like it was February fourteenth. Valentine's Day."

Valentine's Day. I remembered that night. I had laid out a path of candles on the floor of our living room, leading to the dining room table, where I had dinner waiting for David when he got home from work. I remembered what I had cooked: salmon, sautéed spinach, and roasted potatoes. But we had been trying to get pregnant for eleven months. It hadn't occurred to me that anything miraculous might have happened that night.

But since then, Valentine's Day had taken on a special meaning for me. Beyond the Hallmark expectations of flowers and candy, it became a special anniversary. The day when new life began—when my identity as a mother was born and my remarkable daughter's life began to take shape.

That is why it was even more painful that the day that David had called Michaela to tell her we wouldn't adopt Alyana fell on February 14.

Valentine's Day was on a Monday that year, and we had decided the night before. I was still apoplectic with anger and grief, but I had told him that he had veto power over the decision. He told me again and again that he was sorry, that he loved Alyana. And I knew it was true. I remembered the way he read to her before bed, the tenderness with which he carried her in the grocery store, the way they laughed together on the couch when they wore the matching red fireman hats we had in our toy chest.

When David texted me that he had contacted Michaela, I looked at the phone in disbelief. He had really done it.

"But we agreed last night," he said, when I sent a series of angry texts back.

"Yes, but. …"

It took me thirty minutes to complete the reply.

"Don't you know what today is? I can't believe you actually did it today. Of all days."

When I got home, there was a card waiting for me on the bed. A Hafiz quotation was on the front: "Your heart and my heart are very old friends."

Inside were David's words:

> *I know on Valentine's Day you are supposed to show your love by what you can give, and not by taking away a heart's desire. As Hafiz says, love is a mysterious and long road. I hope to find many gifts to share with you on the road of our lives. Your breaking heart breaks mine, and your joy lifts me as well. If I could, I would lift you to the moon and back, and I am sorry I am so small, and only have my small arms to offer. They are always there to love and comfort you.*

* * *

I appreciated David's sweetness, but it didn't diminish my grief and anger. How do you find peace in a marriage in the face of intractable conflict and loss? When no one has done anything wrong? When people just want different things? I had been fighting and suffering over the issue of whether to have another child for more than ten years, as long as Lila had been alive. For all that time, I had been disbelieving, sad, dissatisfied, resentful. First, when I couldn't convince David to have another biological baby, and then again, when he made the decision to let Alyana go. Yet during the same period, there had also been tremendous joy and gratitude in our marriage and in both of our lives. I had been filled, and in many, many ways, I had been enlarged. During that period, I had embraced and been embraced by God in the Trinity, through Jesus and the Holy Spirit, and been baptized. I had discovered vocations and followed through on them, including my vocations as a writer and a foster parent.

So the question continued to hang heavy and huge between us: Now that Alyana was truly gone, what was the way to find peace in our marriage, to find real resolution? To finally put this conflict to rest?

I realized that my vision of resolution, of redemption, was for the bad feelings to go away. I wanted the anger and disappointment to end. I wanted the remaining resentment to drain away like water soaking into the ground until the earth is dry and all trace of moisture is gone.

Yet I realized that perhaps—at least in the short-term—this was unrealistic and not necessary. Instead, perhaps I had to accept the duality of my experience to find the peace I was seeking. Maybe loving David—fully loving our marriage and our lives together—was about accepting all the feelings that exist between us, including the difficult ones. Not expecting that I'd work though the anger until it was gone and I could "move on," but instead embracing the mosaic of experiences that comprised our life and history together.

As the months passed and Valentine's Day approached again, I wondered what I should do that year. Should I forgive and return to romance and candles, even if my heart was not ready to do so? Should I seek revenge by trying to hurt David in some small way? The latter seems ridiculous and wrong, of course, but it was still tempting.

Another possibility came to mind. I am not an artist, but I felt a desire to get a large canvas and make a painting that represented the full mosaic of our lives. I imagined starting with the outline of a large heart in heavy, dark paint. In the upper left corner would be the golden heart for the day when we conceived Lila. In the lower right would be a black heart of losing Alyana. In the center would be the light green grass in the meadow the day David proposed, when we agreed that we would marry and not just be "deeply engaged." And then throughout the rest of the space, all the pieces of living that comprised our marriage and lives together. Mundane, everyday moments. Coaching Soren through homework assignments; remodeling our house; adopting our two cats; countless moments of irritability over the years; lying in bed together in the early morning, when the sky was still dark, skin on skin.

Maybe then I would hang up the painting where everyone could see it. It would be a visible depiction of a life lived together in love and loss, sacrifice and generosity, gratitude and disappointment, anger and acceptance.

When the writer Barbara Brown Taylor was first ordained in the Episcopal church, she realized that wearing her priest's collar always made her stand out in a crowd, and that this demarcation was intentional. She writes, "Being ordained is not about serving God perfectly, but serving God visibly."

We are called to love God and one another visibly. Perhaps this is why, in his second letter to the Corinthians, Paul seems critical of Moses's decision to cover up his face with a veil when his skin shone after he had been speaking with God. Paul writes, "Since then, we have such a hope, we act with great boldness, not like Moses, who put a veil over his face.... Indeed, to this very day whenever Moses is read, a veil lies over their minds, but when one turns to the Lord, the veil is removed....And all of us, with unveiled faces, seeing the glory of the Lord as though reflected in a mirror, are being transformed" (2 Corinthians, 3:12-17).

We are transformed through and with God's love. In this process, our love is made visible. The veils fall away, and everyone can see our shining faces—even when, in our humanness, our love is messy and imperfect.

* * *

When I was pregnant with Lila, we were alarmed when

I started bleeding in the middle of my second trimester. The doctor realized that I had a fibroid that threatened the viability of the pregnancy. They were concerned that the fibroid could cause the cervix to open too soon, and I would miscarry or labor would come too early. Having a fibroid like that during pregnancy was uncommon; the specialist we were referred to at the hospital had never dealt with a case like mine. He consulted with his mentor, who had retired five years previously. That man recommended surgery. So when I was twenty weeks pregnant with Lila, I went in for the procedure. It was a simple process; they would go in vaginally and snip the stem of the fibroid, hoping it would recede through the cervix and that would be the end of it.

All went well. The procedure was successful. What if they hadn't done it, we all wondered later. What if my red-haired, brilliant, beautiful, quiet, funny, thoughtful, loving daughter had never been born?

After the surgery, when I was in the recovery room with David and my mother, I slowly regained feelings in my legs as the anesthesia wore off. David helped me into the bathroom, guiding me out of the bed and holding my arm as I made my way into the tiled room and lowered myself onto the toilet.

Days later, my mother commented on that moment. "He took care of you with such tenderness and unselfconsciousness. He didn't hesitate for a moment. He followed you right into the bathroom. It was totally natural."

I was surprised at the surprise in her voice. Wouldn't

any husband have done the same?

"I don't know why the interaction was so striking to me," my mother continued. "Something about the way he held you up. He loves you so much."

That moment, too, would be included in our mosaic, in the ways that our love was made visible in the world. Together, in the bathroom, on the slippery tile floor. Wearing the cheap hospital socks they gave me, and the thin, papery gown. David's touch on my arm. His love— our love—holding me up, even as I moved forward on unsteady legs.

Epilogue

I STOOD IN FRONT OF THE GLASS DOORS at the Women's Hospital at UNC in Chapel Hill. It was nine o'clock at night, and the doors were locked. I had forgotten that after dark you have to enter the building through the main entrance around the corner, in the Children's Hospital.

I looked through the glass. A janitor was waxing the floor with a large machine. A few people sat in the waiting room. A receptionist was behind the large desk, flipping through a magazine.

I had just come from a nearby church. Two months before, my first memoir had been published, and that evening I had spoken to a small group about the topic of discernment. The church was several blocks from the hospital, and on my way home I impulsively pulled into the large circular driveway and parked my car in front of the main door. Now I was standing on the sidewalk, looking at the building.

Gazing up, I thought about Lila's birth. We had arrived at the hospital just before midnight on Halloween, and she had been born the next morning, on All Saint's Day. I thought about the night, several years later, when I sat in the waiting room in the neonatal intensive care unit at two o'clock in the morning. One of my best friends had an emergency C-section earlier that evening; her son had been born seven weeks early. Just this past week, my friend's son had been diagnosed with autism. I thought about the text message I had received from my brother that afternoon. He lived in New York, and his wife was pregnant with their first child. The results from the prenatal testing they had done that week looked good, he had written. The doctor had confirmed her due date was early April; the baby would likely arrive around Easter.

I thought about all the ways our adult lives unfold in ways we expect and don't expect. The joys and gifts, the losses and disappointments, the surprises, the grief, the growth, the finding resolution and losing it again. I realized, standing there, that I didn't know where Alyana had been born. It could have been at this hospital, or just as easily, somewhere else. Again, I was struck by the emotional juxtaposition of feeling that Alyana is a child of my heart and also recognizing that so much of her past, and most likely all of her future, do not belong to me.

I stood on the sidewalk and realized that I am being

called to give birth in many ways, in ways I never could have imagined when I was younger. I never planned to write books, and publishing the first one felt like launching a child into the world.

I decided in that moment that I wanted to donate a copy of the memoir to the hospital. I had a few extra copies in my car left over from the talk that night. I looked around. The door was locked. Was it worth walking all the way around to the other entrance? And once I got in, who could I give it to? Would I hand it to the receptionist on the night shift? I paused. Maybe this was a dumb idea. I didn't even know if this hospital had a library.

Just then, a nurse in scrubs appeared, walking toward me on the sidewalk. She was heading toward the cancer hospital, and as she approached, I could see the word *surgery* stitched on her chest. Her pace was relaxed; she didn't seem like she was in a hurry, so I stepped toward her.

"Excuse me. I'm sorry to bother you." I inhaled. This seemed silly. "I'm sorry, it's just…well, I just published a book, and I just had an impulse to donate a copy to the hospital. But the door is locked, and I wondered if you could take it inside for me. I mean, well, I guess I should ask first, does the hospital even have a library?"

"Yes, we have a library." She nodded, smiling.

"Okay, well, great. It's just that my daughter was born at this hospital. And I really wanted to have another baby, but it didn't happen. And the book is kind of like a baby for me." The words came out fast, and suddenly I was crying.

I felt embarrassed. Not only was I accosting this stranger

with an odd request, now I was weeping as I stood there on the sidewalk next to her.

But the woman took me into her arms and hugged me. "That's wonderful. Of course the book is your baby. I would be honored to bring it inside for you."

I put my head down on her shoulder and hugged her back. "Thank you. Thank you for understanding. You're my angel tonight."

We parted, and she waved as I drove off, holding the book against her chest.

The next day at church was the Feast of Saint Michael and All Angels. During the sermon, the priest said, "I am absolutely certain that I have seen a few angels in my life. The first one was when I was ten years old. I was alone in the hospital, with appendicitis. My mother had to go home to be with my two younger brothers, and my father was away, traveling for work. We were new in town, and we had no family nearby. I would have to stay in the hospital by myself, all night. I was scared. A janitor at the hospital came in around eleven. He pulled up a chair and sat down. He ended up sitting beside me all night. I knew with certainty that he was an angel."

The coincidence of the story—the hospital, a staff member showing up unexpectedly—felt weighty as I thought back to the nurse the night before. Do we all appear to one another as angels? To give, receive, bless, be blessed by one another?

That night, I thought about Candace, Alyana's birth mother, who had three children, none of whom lived with her now. Jacqueline told us that after Kaila's birth, she had gotten her tubes tied. Candace was in her early thirties and wouldn't have any more children. Michaela told her that the courts had terminated Candace's parental rights earlier that month. What did her future hold?

I thought about Jacqueline. We had talked on the phone just that week. She said she still felt horrible about giving up Alyana and Kaila.

"I'm still fighting my demons to make peace with the decision. I just couldn't be there for them the way they needed. I wasn't enough. I still feel like I failed."

She and Charles had moved to the beach to live with Jacqueline's elderly mother. Her divorce with Mike would probably go through by the end of the year.

"The lawyer is really good, " Jacqueline said. "She's a bulldog. I'm hopeful that things will work out for us."

She would be coming into town to visit Alyana and Kaila later in the month. We made plans to visit, and I was excited to see her and Charles.

I thought about Joan and Keith slogging through the day-to-day of parenting. Dealing with behavior problems and tantrums. Packing lunches, driving to school and daycare twice a day. Making dinners, giving baths, comforting, reprimanding, setting limits. Enjoying the moments of poignancy and sweetness—Halloween costumes and Saturday morning snuggles. Taking Alyana to weekly therapy to help her, perhaps, begin to process the loss and upheaval she had experienced in her short life. Michaela reported that Alyana never wanted to talk much in therapy, but they remained hopeful that it might help. She was still having huge and regular meltdowns.

We hadn't seen them in almost a year. We didn't know whether or when we ever would. I knew that at any time we might bump into them in the grocery store. It seems inevitable in our small town. When we do, I don't know if we'll greet them like family or if we should hold back and be more reserved. I don't know if there's any hope that we will be part of Alyana's life in the short- or long-term.

In the meantime, the question I get from people most often—constantly, in fact—is whether we will do it again. Will we foster another child?

I don't know. Beyond the emotional risk it would involve, beyond the fatigue we all feel after the events of the past three years, beyond the remaining questions about whether there is space in our lives as my career continues to hurtle forward, demanding more and more of me, there is a bigger question. Is it right to welcome a child into one's house temporarily if one cannot commit to the possibility of adoption if the child ends up needing a permanent home?

I know a woman who has done just that, beautifully and generously, for years. She has fostered twelve children, and her policy is that she will not adopt. Seven of the kids have returned to their biological families, and five have been adopted by others. She is nurturing and loves the children fiercely while they are in her home. Then she lets them go. But she is in her late sixties, and each time she explains to the child that she is a grandmother, and the child deserves younger parents.

In contrast, wouldn't a child in our home look at Lila and our relative youth and inevitably feel rejected if we sent them off again after being in our home for an extended period of time? Wouldn't we represent just one more abandonment? Ideally, it seems that foster families need to be willing to make the ultimate sacrifice of loving—equally willing to let a child go if it is decided they should return to their family of origin, and at the same time, remain open to adoption if there's a need for them to stay. But the world isn't perfect, and this seems like an impossible expectation—that foster families could rise to such generosity, open-heartedness, and flexibility, even as they deal with the day-to-day stresses and joys and demands of parenting.

Perhaps the best we can do is to learn, and then role model, how to both love deeply and be able to let go without becoming bitter in the process.

The poet Mary Oliver writes:

> *To live in this world,*
> *you must be able to do three things:*
> *to love what is mortal;*
> *to hold it against your bones*
> *knowing your own life depends on it; and,*
> *when the time comes to let it go,*
> *to let it go.*
>
> —*In Blackwater Woods*

An experienced foster parent once told me that signing up for the job is volunteering to get your heart broken. Despite all of the heartache, I remain incredibly thankful for the time we had with Alyana. Even with the hole that Alyana's absence had left in our hearts and in our lives, I somehow felt more whole because of the experience of loving her.

Thinking back to the class we took to get licensed as foster parents, I remember the social worker warning us to be mindful of our motivations before we committed to the process. She told us that we should only foster if we were there to help the kids, not to meet an unfulfilled need in our own lives. Of course, this makes sense. Most children in foster care have gone through unspeakable horrors of violence or neglect. Their needs must come first. And yet it is undeniable that loving Alyana—even though I lost her in the process— met a deep need in me. A need to parent, to love, to bind my life and heart to another child. It gave me the unexpected opportunity to be connected to others in Alyana's extended family, whom I otherwise would never have known. When I talk to Jacqueline on the phone now, she still jokes that I'm her "sister from another mister."

When David and I became foster parents, my jumbled motivations at the outset *were* largely selfish. I knew that then, and I know that now. Yet I also know that when we "help" someone, it often becomes a mutual ministry. That ministry occurs through loving one another.

There were so many moments of grace and love during the time when Alyana was with us. Sitting on our back deck, blowing soap bubbles and giggling with her in the afternoon sun. Bringing her on the vacation we took in

Vermont, soon after she arrived. Watching my parents and brothers fall in love with her overnight, just as I had. Having the chance to tuck another sweet girl into bed at night. Through the process, something in me was healed. Is that selfish? I don't know, but I am thankful that I had the chance to do all of those things. I'm grateful that, for a while, Alyana was my girl, and I was her mom.

David feels the same way. I asked him recently if he was glad that we became foster parents.

"Of course." He looked surprised at the question. "I love Alyana deeply. It was worth it."

Hearing this, I felt something in me relax. I was thankful to know he didn't regret it.

"I mean, think about it," he continued. "There is no cost to loving freely. The pain we've experienced has nothing to do with the love we feel. Our job is to love without grasping or holding on."

A few minutes after he said this, he grabbed Lila and started wrestling her. She shrieked as he lowered her to the floor. She giggled and tried to wriggle away, but he grabbed her leg and pulled her back to the center of the rug.

Over the years, I had watched him go through this routine with our kids—Soren, Lila, and Alyana—hundreds of times. Crouched in the middle of our living room, David and Lila were backlit by the sun coming through the window. From my seat on the couch, watching them laugh, I noticed how their skin seemed to shine.

Acknowledgements

First, I want to thank David for allowing me to share our story—his generosity, wisdom, patience, and love throughout this process continue to amaze and inspire me. I am also incredibly grateful to my stepson, Soren, and our daughter, Lila, for embarking on the foster care journey with us, even though it was not their idea in the first place. I am very proud of the kindness, understanding, and love they both demonstrated every step of the way. I am also tremendously grateful to my parents, Bruce and Lynn Holbein, to whom this book is partly dedicated. Their support, encouragement, and love mean more than I can possibly say. I am also very thankful for the support we received from our entire extended family while we were fostering. I'm especially grateful to my brothers,

Chris and Andrew, and my sisters-in-law, Angela and Eva; my cousins Laura and John; my aunt Tina; David's parents and stepmother, Pam, Paul and Kathy; and David's siblings, Kristen and Tom, and our sister-in-law, Stacy.

There are so many friends who supported us during the foster care journey, and as I was writing this book. I want to especially thank Caroline and Brian Pence, Erica Witsell, Steve Erickson, Kat Tumlinson, Mehul Patel, Trinity Zan, Lucy Wilson, Tricia Petruney, Elsie Kagan, Karen Stegman, Alyson Grine, Micha Josephy, Kelly McCoy, Laura Gallaher, Krista, Peter and Joshua Alexander, Grace Foley, Mia Irwin, Tori Ralston, Robert Malik Lawrence, Kirsten Krueger, Ismail Suayah, Krista Bremer, Carol McGuire, Sonia Katchian, Mary Rushing, Wayne Cherry, and Stacye Leanza. I am also thankful for my coworkers for their support especially Laneta Dorflinger, Rebecca Callahan and Aurélie Brunie.

I am enormously grateful to the Rev. Liz Dowling-Sendor, who serves as my spiritual director and who provided incredible support and guidance throughout the entire period of discernment, fostering, and writing. I am thankful to the Rev. Wren Blessing for her friendship and for (unintentionally!) providing the inspiration for this book's title as part of the sermon she gave years ago. I am incredibly grateful to the clergy and laity at Church of the Holy Family including the Rev. Dr. Clarke French, Rev. Sarah Ball-Damberg, Rev. Angela Nelson, and the prayer team for the love and guidance they provided to me and my family during this journey. I am also thankful to members of the Kosala Mahayana Buddhist Center, especially Ethan Lechner, Wendy Webber, and Ann Gerhardt. Our foster daughter was welcomed with open arms at both Church of the Holy Family and the Kosala Center, and she loved both communities.

I am also thankful for the people who provided support as I was editing the manuscript and seeking publication, including Brian Allain, J. Dana Trent, Kristen Lingo, Amanda Martin, and Kathy Izard.

I remain incredibly grateful for the amazing team at Light Messages Publishing, including my wonderful editor, Elizabeth Turnbull.

I also want to express my gratitude to the staff at the Department Social Services in Orange County, North Carolina. I'm especially thankful to Tracy Trask for all the ways she supported us during this entire process. I am grateful to be part of several groups on Facebook that connect foster and adoptive parents around the country; these online groups have provided important opportunities to share experiences and to give and receive support. On any given day, there are over four hundred thousand kids in foster care in the United States. If I've learned anything, it is that no two stories are the same. I do not intend for the publication of this book to suggest that our family's experience is typical or representative of others' experiences. For those who are interested in learning more about foster care or adoption through the foster care system, I encourage you to contact your local social services agency.

Finally, I want to express my deepest thanks to members

of our foster daughter's biological and adoptive families, who gave their blessing for me to pursue publication of this book. I have done my best to change details to protect confidentiality. All profits from book sales will be donated to non-profit organizations working at the local and national levels to support families involved with the foster care system and that have been impacted by chronic poverty or violence.

Notes

Chapter 1

Tugwell, Simon. *Prayer in Practice*. Springfield, IL: Templegate Publishers, 1974.

Nouwen, Henri J. *In the Name of Jesus: Reflections on Christian Leadership*. New York: Crossroad Publishing Company, 1989.

Chapter 2

Fermor, Patrick L. *A Time to Keep Silence*. New York: New York Review Books, 2007 ed. Originally, 1953.

Foster, Richard J. *Celebration of Discipline: The Path to Spiritual Growth*. San Francisco: Harper & Row, 1988.

Houselander, Caryll. *A Child in Winter: Advent, Christmas, and Epiphany with Caryll Houselander*. Edited by Hoffman, Thomas. Franklin, Wisconsin: Sheed & Ward, 2000.

Chapter 3
O'Connor, Flannery. *A Prayer Journal.* New York: Farrar, Straus and Giroux. 2013.

Chapter 4
Bernard of Clairvaux. "Four Degrees of Love." *Devotional Classics: Selected Readings for Individuals and Groups.* Edited by Foster, Richard J and Smith, James B. New York: HarperOne, 2005.

Chapter 5
Stone Roger. "Tillich's Kairos and its Trajectory." Revista Eletrônica Correlatio. 2018: 17(1). https://www.metodista.br/revistas/revistas-ims/index.php/COR/article/view/8980.

Chapter 7
McColman, Carl. *The Big Book of Christian Mysticism: The Essential Guide to Contemplative Spirituality.* San Francisco: Hampton Roads. 2010.

Chapter 8
Borg, Markus J. *Meeting Jesus Again for the First Time.* New York: HarperOne, 1994.

Chapter 14
Houselander, Caryll. *The Reed of God.* New York: Sheed & Ward. 1944.

Hauerwas, Stanley. Sermon. Church of the Holy Family. Chapel Hill, North Carolina. 2016.

Bolz-Weber, Nadia. *Accidental Saints: Finding God in all the Wrong People.* New York: Convergent Books, 2015.

Chapter 17
Swoboda, A. J. Quoting Henri Nouwen in *Subversive Sabbath: the Surprising Power of Rest in a Nonstop World.* Grand Rapids, MI: Brazos Press, 2018.

Chapter 18
McCleneghan, Bromleigh. *Good Christian Sex: Why Chastity Isn't the Only Option—And Other Things the Bible Says About Sex.* New York: HaperOne, 2016.

Chapter 19
Taylor, Barbara Brown. *Leaving Church: A Memoir of Faith.* New York: HaperOne, 2006.

Epilogue
Oliver, Mary. "In Blackwater Woods." *American Primitive.* New York: Back Bay Books, 1983.

About the Author

KATE H. RADEMACHER GREW UP outside of Boston, Massachusetts, and now lives in Chapel Hill, North Carolina, with her family. In her debut memoir, *Following the Red Bird: First steps into a life of faith*, Kate describes how she came to embrace a relationship with God after maintaining a pick-and-choose approach to spirituality for many years. *Their Faces Shone: A foster parent's lessons on loving and letting go* is her second book.

Kate works full-time in international public health, and she is currently working on her third book about the challenges and gifts of maintaining a Sabbath practice in a non-stop world.

Connect with Kate online at:
www.katerademacher.com

If you liked

Their Faces Shone

you might also enjoy these titles from
Light Messages Publishing

Following the Red Bird: First steps into a life of faith
Kate H. Rademacher

Wait: Thoughts and Practice in Waiting on God
Rebecca Brewster Stevenson

The Color of Together: Metaphors of Connectedness
Milton Brasher-Cunningham

Of Green Stuff Woven
Cathleen Bascom

Faith and Air: The Miracle List
Scott Mason

Climbing Lessons
Tim Bascom